DEMOCRACY: HOW DIRECT?

Elliott Abrams, former president of the Ethics and Public Policy Center, is a special assistant to the President and the National Security Council's senior director for democracy, human rights, and international operations. He headed the Center from 1996 to June 2001. He is the author *of Faith or Fear: How Jews Can Survive in a Christian America* and of *Undue Process: A Story of How Political Differences Are Turned into Crimes.*

DEMOCRACY: HOW DIRECT?
Views from the Founding Era and the Polling Era

EDITED BY
Elliott Abrams

ESSAYS BY
Herman Belz, James S. Fishkin, Benjamin Ginsberg,
Charles R. Kesler, Benjamin I. Page, Gary Rosen,
G. Alan Tarr, Ron K. Unz, M. Dane Waters

ROWMAN & LITTLEFIELD PUBLISHERS, INC.
Lanham ▪ Boulder ▪ New York ▪ Oxford
ETHICS AND PUBLIC POLICY CENTER

ROWMAN & LITTLEFIELD PUBLISHERS, INC.
Published in the United States of America by
Rowman & Littlefield, Inc.,
A Member of the Rowman & Littlefield Publishing Group
4720 Boston Way, Lanham, Maryland 20706
www.rowmanlittlefield.com

P.O. Box 317, Oxford OX2 9RU, UK

Co-published with the
ETHICS AND PUBLIC POLICY CENTER
1015 Fifteenth Street NW, Washington, D.C. 20005
www.eppc.org

Copyright © 2002 by the Ethics and Public Policy Center

British Library Cataloguing in Publication information available

Library of Congress Cataloging-in-Publication Data
Democracy—how direct? : views from the founding era and the polling era /
edited by Elliott Abrams; essays by Herman Belz ... [et al.].
     p. cm.
    Includes bibliographical references and index.
    ISBN 0-7425-2318-7 (alk. paper) — ISBN 0-7425-2319-5 (pbk. : alk.
paper)
     1. Democracy—United States—Congresses. 2. Referendum—United
States—Congresses. 3. Representative government and representation—United
States—Congresses. 4. Public opinion—United States—Congresses. I.
Abrams, Elliott, 1948-
    JK1726.D495 2002
    320.973—dc21   2001040934

Printed in the United States of America

♾™The paper used in this publication meets the minimum requirements of American
National Standard for Information Sciences—Permanence of Paper for Printed Library
Materials, ANSI/NISO Z39.48-1992.

Contents

Preface

Elliott Abrams

For more than two hundred years Americans have been debating how direct a democracy they want. Those who have favored a powerful role for direct voting, whereby public opinion dictates public policy, have most feared elitism and the usurpation of democratic rule by combinations of politicians, bureaucrats, and the rich. Those who have favored representative forms over direct voting have most feared that emotion and factional interests would undermine stability and justice. They have viewed representation not as a necessary evil but as a guarantor of responsible government, where cool-headed deliberation within institutions takes the place of popular passion.

In this latter camp were the Founding Fathers. They wanted cool deliberation rather than passion in the handling of public affairs, fearing what Hamilton called "the turbulence and follies of democracy." Madison called for "the total exclusion of the people in their collective capacity" from governing, and most of the framers of the Constitution thought the very democratic state governments were ineffective and their governors weak. But their views, while dominant in the federal Constitution, did not persuade all their contemporaries, and state constitutions often did permit far more direct popular control of public matters and personnel.

This more populist tradition has remained strong in America, and in recent years referendums—for example, California's propositions limiting taxation and barring affirmative action in university admissions, Oregon's initiative permitting medical use of marijuana, Hawaii's vote to bar same-sex marriage, and Alabama's decision against a state lottery—have taken a central place in public policy, bypassing representative institutions. Some proponents of referendums claim that "the people" are far better educated now than they were two hundred years ago; others note that often the subjects of these initiatives call for a moral judgment that legislators are no better situated than other citizens to make.

In August 2000 the Ethics and Public Policy Center convened a conference to examine this two-century-old debate and its contemporary ramifications. Given the Founders' beliefs, our representative political institutions, modern telecommunications technology, and the current understandings of the American people about democracy and public opinion, does direct democracy or representation better reflect public opinion? Do we see today, in this profusion of initiatives and referendums at the state level, a flowering of direct democracy? A failure of state governments to represent voters' views on critical issues? These and related questions of history, political philosophy, and current practice were the subject of the conference and form the substance of this volume.

Gary Rosen and **Charles R. Kesler** first provide historical grounding by laying out the views of the Founders. **Herman Belz** looks at Lincoln and the nineteenth-century view of American democracy. **G. Alan Tarr** reminds us that there is not a single American tradition but rather are there several competing traditions, reflected in the constitutions adopted at the state and federal levels in the late eighteenth and early nineteenth centuries. **James S. Fishkin, Benjamin Ginsberg**, and **Benjamin I. Page** examine polling, public opinion, and the strengths and weaknesses of American democracy today. **M. Dane Waters** describes the current use of the referendum process in the states. And finally, **Ron K. Unz** tells the tale of his own foray into direct democracy in challenging bilingual education in California through a ballot initiative. Those who would dismiss direct voter action as an unnecessary or even dangerous intervention in our representative democracy should ponder Unz's account of a political system unable or unwilling to respond either to voter preferences or to mountains of sociological data.

A glance at Europe shows us that the debate over representation and democracy is still very much under way there also. Decision-making power is sometimes being shifted "up" to Brussels, ever further from the direct control of the citizen, and sometimes "down" to regions (such as Wales or Scotland) below the national level. Although nothing quite so dramatic is happening in the United States, in recent years some highly sensitive public-policy issues have been decided by direct voting in several states, and some state legislatures have taken steps to make future citizen initiatives more difficult and therefore less likely.

The suspicion that representative government too seldom reflects the people's real views, and the counter-suspicion that direct popular voting will lead to excesses of passion and deficits of deliberation, remain in the air. The debate over direct democracy appears to be a permanent part of our political culture. The essays that follow will, we trust, help to raise the level of this debate with their valuable combination of historical analysis, contemporary data, and theoretical understanding.

CHAPTER ONE

The Founders' Views of Direct Democracy and Representation

Charles R. Kesler

"No taxation without representation" was one of the most important slogans of the American Revolution. "No taxation without direct democracy" was not. Why not?

In today's parlance, "direct democracy" refers especially to those devices such as the initiative, referendum, and recall that involve citizens directly in lawmaking or that reduce the independence of elected officials by subjecting them to citizens' peremptory control. The term includes the direct primary election, the now prevalent means for exerting voters' sway over the nomination of presidential and other political candidates. Efforts to abolish the Electoral College, not to mention the successful movement early last century to switch from indirect to direct election of U.S. senators, also come under the rubric of direct democracy. In an extended sense, opinion polling and other tools of the modern political campaign (and increasingly of modern political governance) are elements of direct democracy, too, insofar as they imply that savvy

---

Charles R. Kesler is professor of government at Claremont McKenna College and director of the Henry Salvatori Center for the Study of Individual Freedom in the Modern World. He is the editor of *The Claremont Review of Books*. His revision of Clinton Rossiter's 1961 edition of *The Federalist Papers*, with a new introduction and notes, was published in 1999. Currently he is editing and contributing to a book of essays on the political thought of American Progressivism.

politicians should always be prepared to truckle to popular opinion. And on the horizon, computers and the Internet promise—perhaps threaten would be a better word—to link citizens and government together in a brave new world of teledemocracy or cyberdemocracy.

In fact, enthusiasts for direct democracy commonly assume that the future belongs to their cause, that as citizens become more and better educated they will be increasingly competent to govern themselves directly, and will be keen to do so. Even if the capacity and the desire for direct democracy do not go exactly hand in hand, the fact remains that modern citizens are used to making more and more choices for themselves, and this habit encourages them to believe that the line from personal to public choice is straight and easy.

Progressive Arguments

This confidence that the future should, and will, be increasingly democratic recalls the Progressives, who at the turn of the twentieth century invented direct democracy as we know it. It was the Progressives, impatient with the established forms of American government, who first proposed that these forms, including the Constitution itself, be thoroughly renovated in the name of democracy and efficiency.

To be sure, the Progressives championed direct democracy not as a substitute for representative government but rather as a corrective for its abuses, which had accumulated as America's political system, the very best the eighteenth century could offer, suffered the strains and indignities of American life in the late nineteenth and early twentieth centuries. Although the principles of the Constitution were no help in this crisis (indeed, were part of the problem, according to most Progressives), the innovative spirit of its framers and, still more, the democratic spirit of '76 could nonetheless be invoked as precedents. This was helpful, at least rhetorically. None of the captains of Progressivism doubted that the cure for the ills of American democracy was more democracy; but they were relieved to discover, or at least to pretend, that the needed democratic transfusions could be obtained from compatible donors, and that nothing un-American was involved.[1] If perchance something foreign were required, however, it could be Americanized or by other methods and arguments be rendered tolerable to the body politic.[2]

Their advocates thus defended the initiative, recall, and especially the referendum as new installments of a democratic legacy stretching back at least to John Calvin and his Puritan followers in New England, and probably all the way back to the Saxon *witenagemote* and the Teutonic *folkmoot*, two forms of what Charles Sumner Lobingier called "primitive popular assemblies."[3] Whether derived from religious doctrines or "race inheritance," the American genius for democracy, argued the Progressives, had proved adaptable to changing times and social conditions so that it was possible to speak of "the evolution of democracy and direct legislation" and to trace the overall growth of "popular participation in law-making."[4] The new institutions of direct democracy were needed to continue this advance and to consolidate what had already been won.

In the words of one of its Progressive admirers, Lewis Jerome Johnson, "direct legislation" is a safeguard "not only . . . against mob rule, but against the only thing likely with us to lead to violent revolution, namely, machine rule for the benefit of the privileged few." In fact, Johnson concluded upon reading the "sturdy New England doctrines" of John Adams and the framers of the Massachusetts constitution that "the only reason why the fathers did not then and there establish direct legislation for the state" was its physical impossibility. "They knew no more of railways than Caesar did, [and] such highways as they had were not so good as Caesar's." Given "the telegraph, high-speed printing press, and the railway," said Johnson, Americans could now proceed "from the point where the fathers were forced to stop and can vindicate more clearly than ever the soundness of their noble idealism." The initiative and referendum, he boasted, "appeal particularly to progressive Americans in whom still lives the spirit of the liberty-loving men who founded this nation."[5]

Direct Democracy in the Founding Era

As a matter of fact, the American founders were in various ways acquainted with direct democracy. The New Englanders among them were intimately familiar with it, having grown up with town meetings, those democratic assemblies that seized Tocqueville's imagination and fascinated the Progressives as well. Compared to the initiative and referendum, the town meeting was a more fundamental type of direct democracy in which the citizens assembled in person to conduct the government, or at the least to enact law and pronounce important decisions. Here the citizens taxed themselves, managed the town school, elected magistrates, set the pastor's salary, provided poor relief, and in some cases acted as a court, trying offenders and deciding probate questions.[6]

Another kind of popular participation in lawmaking became known to Americans after 1778, when in Massachusetts the proposed "Frame of Government," written by the state legislature, was sent for ratification to the citizens in their town meetings. This constitution was rejected, largely on the grounds that, having been composed by the Assembly or General Court, it lacked the people's authority. A new constitution was drafted by the state's—and the nation's—first constitutional convention, called especially for the purpose, and this document, the Constitution of 1780, was approved by the citizens and is still in force today. New Hampshire followed its neighbor's example, submitting to its citizens a constitution that was rejected in 1779, another rejected in 1782, and a third that was ratified in 1783.[7] Similarly, the Massachusetts legislature in 1777 sent the proposed federal Articles of Confederation to the towns for discussion and approval, which it secured in due course; and the New Hampshire legislature sought similar though apparently more informal soundings of public opinion regarding the Articles.[8]

Despite these interesting episodes, direct democracy in the founding era had definite limits. The tradition of town meetings did not extend beyond New England because towns as a governmental unit did not extend beyond New England.[9] Besides, and more to the point, everyone agreed that most and probably all of the states of the American union were too large and populous to be governed by citizen-assemblies of the kind possible in Ipswich or Athens.[10] And though the Massachusetts constitutional convention quickly became a widely imitated model, its practice of seeking popular ratification of the resulting plan of government was not widely copied. "The fact remains," as Charles Lobingier put it, "that less than one-fourth of the state constitutions during the first forty-five years of our national existence were actually voted on by the people." Only after 1820, and more markedly after 1831, did popular ratification of state constitutions became routine.[11] When the proposed Constitution of the United States emerged from the Philadelphia Convention in 1787, it was sent for ratification (in keeping with the provisions of Article VII) to specially called state conventions, not directly to the people.

Even so, were the Progressives right in thinking that there was nothing in the "noble idealism" of the "liberty-loving" American founders that was inconsistent with direct democracy? I think not. In the first place, the Progressives' vision of direct democracy is not simply an up-to-date version of a New England town meeting. Suffice it to say that there were no Ph.D.s present in those old town meetings. For the Progressives, direct democracy is always directed democracy, only it must be the experts (i.e., the Progressives), not the rich, who do the directing. This is the common theme in the calls a hundred years ago for "democracy and efficiency" and in today's seminars on how to make direct democracy and "deliberative democracy" coincide. Of course, the many are not capable of judging the expertness of the experts, and so in the decisive sense the experts are unaccountable to the people. This problem is exacerbated by the Progressives' characteristic appeal to a kind of wisdom—social scientific and historicist wisdom—that in their view transcends and trumps the Constitution.

In the second place, the Founders, as we shall see, distrusted direct democracy precisely because it could not be kept deliberative and because it displayed an unfortunate tendency to become tyrannical. John Adams, who was thoroughly familiar with the virtues of town meetings, saw deeply into their vices as well. "If by *the people* is meant all the inhabitants of a single city," he wrote, "they are not in a general assembly, at all times, the best keepers of their own liberties, nor perhaps at any time, unless you separate from them the executive and judicial power, and temper their authority in legislation with the maturer counsels of the one and the few."[12] For these and other reasons, Adams and most of the other Founders rejected direct democracy as the best form of government.

What they favored instead was republican government, featuring bicameralism, representation, and separation of powers—in short, the features of American constitutionalism defended by *The Federalist*. The test of good government was not, in the Founders' view, merely democratic willfulness or purity but also the securing of private rights and the public good. In republican government, the few (the talented, the wealthy, the ambitious, the virtuous) were free to make their political contributions to the common good through the forms of representative government—either by standing for office or by being appointed by officials who were themselves elected. In either case, the few would be accountable to the people and to the Constitution; and their "counsels" were counsels of prudence, not of technical expertise.

In the nineteenth century, Americans began commonly to refer to their republican government as democracy, and we continue to call it that today. But our "representative democracy" or "constitutional democracy" is a very different thing from direct democracy, in spirit and in substance.[13]

RULING VERSUS REPRESENTATION

That direct democracy in the purest sense was impracticable outside of New England towns did not mean, of course, that it did not carry moral authority among Americans of the founding era. Direct democracy could still function, and did so for many prominent Americans, as a touchstone for republican government, an ideal to be approximated. We shall soon enough enter this debate at its culmination, the dispute over ratification of the U.S. Constitution. But first we should examine briefly the issue underlying the whole founding-era discussion: politics conceived as ruling versus politics conceived as representation.

As an alternative to all forms of representative government, there was a possibility hardly raised by anyone in the founding period: ruling, in the old-fashioned Aristotelian sense. For Aristotle, politics was organized around regimes, and every regime was the rule of a part of the city over the whole—the rule of one, or few, or many over everyone else. In asserting its claim to rule, a part of the body politic had to impose on the whole community its partisan view of what was just and good. If the rulers looked to their own selfish good, then the resulting regimes were bad; these were the regimes of tyranny, oligarchy, and what Aristotle called democracy. If the rulers looked instead to the common good of the city, then the resulting regimes were good— kingship, aristocracy, and what Aristotle called polity.[14] The latter term, in Greek *politeia*, is also the generic word for "regime" and in Latin was rendered *res publica*, "republic." Thus for Aristotle and those who followed him, the good form of rule by the many may be called republican government, as opposed to democracy, the unjust or selfish form of popular rule. This distinction is important to bear in mind, because it underlay many of the American founders' discussions and was revived, as we shall see, in a slightly different form by James Madison in his criticism of "pure democracy."

When the ruling part imposed its view of who should rule and why on the community, it shaped a whole way of life for the city and its citizens. Accordingly, contemporary communitarians like to claim Aristotle as one of their own because of his assurance that political activity can mold a community's habits and moral aspirations. But for Aristotle, politics was not the easy harmony but typically the conflict of opinions about who should rule—about whose city this is, about what kind of community it should be. For Aristotle, the ruling opinions of society were basically the opinions of the ruling class. Nonetheless, the rulers' authority could always be questioned and usually was. Regimes therefore tended to be unstable, because their ruling opinion was partisan, i.e., partial, hence disputable. Even the good regimes were ripe for degeneration because their rulers' opinions and actions were not immune to challenge. As Plato expressed it, every actual city was really two cities, the city of the rich (the oligarchic regime) and the city of the poor (the democratic), and the two were constantly at war.[15]

The Mixed Regime

In theory or in speech, the solution to this perpetual civil war, to its instability and alternating injustice, was political philosophy, which tried to ascend from opinions about justice to knowledge of justice. But political philosophers had, as it were, fewer divisions even than the pope (though neither's long-term victories should be underestimated!), and so in practice the best solution to the partisan limits of rule was the mixed regime, which forced partisans to share power and encouraged them to admit that their adversaries were not all wrong. Aristotle called the mixed regime *politeia*, "polity," the same Greek word he had used to describe the good form of popular government, i.e., the republican regime. Thus began a venerable confusion concerning the relation between republican and mixed governments. Most republican governments were mixed regimes, but not all mixed governments were (or were considered) republican.[16]

Modern representative institutions of government arose from the medieval form of the mixed regime, particularly as it developed in England. One, few, and many were here translated into king, lords, and commoners, each a part of the body politic and each with its own piece of justice. But the medieval House of Commons was not like the Roman *comitia*, an assembly of all the citizens or commoners; the House of Commons was a representative institution. Yet it did not represent individual commoners as such. It represented them as a class, as an estate of the realm, and so as an aid or a check to ruling. English government as a whole was not representative; to make an obvious point, the king and the lords did not gain their authority by the consent of the governed. In the words of Harvey C. Mansfield, Jr., the people were a part "to be represented *to* their government," not "to be represented *by* their government." The institutions of the medieval mixed regime sought "to prevent tyranny by one authority," but they did not "serve to limit all authority to the protection of private liberty." Over time, the balance within England's mixed regime shifted as the Commons asserted itself more and more. The Constitution became less medieval and more modern, and (what is not the same thing) less monarchical and more republican, but the word "republican," especially after the unhappy experience of the Puritan Commonwealth, remained for most loyal British subjects in the eighteenth century a hateful term.[17]

Representative institutions are medieval, then, but the theory of representation in the American founding is not; it is one of the "improvements" in the science of politics lauded in *Federalist* No. 9.[18] For the Americans, the Declaration of Independence proclaimed the foundations of representative government when it announced that the "just powers" of government were derived from "the consent of the governed," i.e., the people, who were by nature free and equal. Decent government should both "secure these [individual] rights" and "effect their [the people's] safety and happiness." Government must represent each individual and, at the same time, the whole people, the people composed of consenting individuals. In order to serve both private rights and the public good, government must rest on *consent*, not on the *opinion* of those consenting as to whose claim to rule is better. Government is thus *essentially* representative: rather than the rule of a part over the whole, it represents each individual's claim, on the basis of natural right, to rule himself. One, few, and many are dissolved into individuals and then recombined into "the people."

The source of all political authority might thus seem to be the people, the whole people, and nothing but the people. But this is misleading. The "right of the people" is itself grounded on the self-evident truth "that all men are created equal," and the Declaration insists on viewing the rights of man in light of man's relation—in the decisive sense his inferiority—and consequent duty to God.[19] To appeal to the most prominent example: the signers of the Declaration invoke their "sacred honor" in pledging their lives and fortunes in support of American and human liberty, which they honor as part of a natural and God-given endowment that they are obliged to use, not abuse. To take a more subtle example: while God in his perfection may combine legislative, judicial, and executive powers in the same hands ("the laws of nature and of nature's God," "the Supreme Judge of the world," "Divine Providence"), human beings may not.

And so George III is taken to task for violating, among other things, the separation of powers and particularly for threatening "the right of representation in the Legislature, a right inestimable to them [the people] and formidable to tyrants only." An "inestimable" right is one whose worth is beyond calculation, a right worthy of noble sacrifice. And so in the Declaration of Independence, man's natural rights are understood not merely as means to secure life or comfortable life but also as means to, and indeed elements of, an honorable human life. Representative government pursuant to these rights is, therefore, itself an "inestimable" right of the "good people of these colonies." Although opposed to every form of the divine right of kings, the republicanism based on the Declaration understands itself to be obedient to natural and divine law.

REPRESENTATIVE GOVERNMENT IN THE FOUNDING

The Founders' views of the optimal form of representative government gradually clarified in the course of a quarter-century's debate, which began over the question of taxation without representation. Responding to the Stamp Act, James Otis in 1764 argued that the solution to the problem was obvious—"an American representation in Parliament." (He admitted, however, that "a subordinate legislative among themselves" would judge better about taxes than the imperial Parliament.)[20] Their British opponents retorted that the American colonists were already represented in Parliament. No Americans were actually "electors," of course, with the right to vote for members of the House of Commons. But the Americans were "virtually" represented, inasmuch as the Americans were commoners and there was a House of Commons. The Americans who bemoaned their lack of representation were variously merchants, manufacturers, freeholders, and (most vociferously) lawyers—but lo there were merchants, manufacturers, freeholders, and lawyers in the Commons, faithfully representing the interests of their fellows across the sea. In short, virtual representation under the British Constitution was a form of non-elective representation that presumed a more or less class-based society and a static economy. Great Britain itself resembled such a quasi-feudal society less and less, and virtual representation had been under bitter attack in Britain for more than a century.

Americans rejected the theory even more emphatically. Daniel Dulany in 1765 denounced the notion of virtual representation of the colonies as "a mere cobweb, spread to catch the unwary and entangle the weak." Why? Unlike the inhabitants of Britain, Americans could not become electors (e.g., by moving to a different borough); Americans lacked the "inseparable connection" between non-electors and electors that obtained in Britain because the laws applied equally to both (taxes there affected electors and non-electors alike, but Parliament's taxes on American non-electors affected electors in Britain not at all); and Americans lacked what Dulany shrewdly identified as the motherland's "necessity of imagining a double or virtual representation to avoid iniquity and absurdity," because the Americans were perfectly capable of taxing themselves in their own legislatures. So the Americans were neither actually nor virtually represented in Parliament, and the Commons of Britain could not give and grant supplies on behalf of the Commons of America.[21]

Dulany conceded that virtual representation made sense, or at least more sense, in Britain itself, or wherever there was that "inseparable connection" between the interests of electors and the interests of non-electors. And the Americans continued to invoke virtual representation to justify the fact that women (especially wives) and children could be legislated for and even taxed without their express consent. But the gravamen of their argument placed active or elective representation at the heart of just government, and on questions not merely of taxation but of legislation as well. If legislatures were to resist, in the words of the Declaration, "with manly firmness" any "invasions on the rights of the people," they needed to inspire and to enjoy the people's active confidence. If "no taxation without representation" was the battle cry, then justice must demand not merely consent in the origination of government but also continual consent to government's operations.

The Role of Elective Representation

What role, then, should elective representation play in popular or republican government? The question was highly contested between the advocates and the critics of the proposed United States Constitution. In her useful study *The Concept of Representation*, Hanna Pitkin distinguishes two accounts of representation, which she calls the mandate and the independence theories.[22] The critics of the Constitution, the so-called Anti-Federalists, adhered, in general, to a version of the mandate theory, as did most of the writers of the state constitutions in the 1770s and early 1780s. According to this view, the representative's task is to mirror the views of his constituents. By contrast, the Federalists defended a version of the independence theory, which sees the representative as a trustee who owes his constituents his own best judgment about their interests and the public good. (The classic statement of the latter viewpoint is Edmund Burke's 1774 post-election speech to the electors of Bristol.[23])

For example, the "Federal Farmer," one of the soberest Anti-Federalist writers, defined "a full and equal representation of the people in the legislature" as "that which possesses the same interests, feelings, opinions, and views the people themselves would were they all assembled." He assumed, furthermore, that the people are divided into "orders," that a "fair representation" would provide "that every order of men in the community, according to the common course of elections, can have a share in it," and that "in order to allow professional men, merchants, traders, farmers, mechanics, etc. to bring a just proportion of their best informed men respectively into the legislature, the representation must be considerably numerous," which the proposed House of Representatives was not.[24]

"Brutus," another leading Anti-Federalist writer, echoed the point. "The very term *representative* implies, that the person or body chosen for this purpose should resemble those who appoint them—a representation of the people of America, if it be a true one, must be like the people. . . . [The representatives] are the sign—the people are the thing signified."[25] Anti-Federalist semiotics thus came close to a form of proportional representation (one could even say virtual representation) familiar to us today in the desire of recent presidential administrations to form a cabinet or a whole government "that looks like the American people." Of course, the Anti-Federalists were thinking not in terms of racial and identity politics but in the categories of old-fashioned political economy.

In any event, the mandate or mirror theory implies a certain affinity between representation and direct democracy. If it were possible to assemble the whole people, after all, representation would be unnecessary. But this was not possible, given the scale of late eighteenth-century American political life; and if it *had* been possible, its consequences would have been dismal. During the debate over the proposed Massachusetts constitution of 1778, a number of towns in Essex County dispatched delegates to a convention, which reported back unfavorably on the document. Their conclusions were written up in the so-called *Essex Result*, which, reviewing the possibility of direct democracy at the state level, predicted: "Sixty-thousand people could not discuss with candor, and determine with deliberation. Tumults, riots, and murder would be the result."[26]

It must be admitted, however, that the Anti-Federalists would probably be startled by the notion that they stood for direct democracy. They thought that the "natural aristocrats" were as naturally a part of the republican citizen-body as the democrats, and they tended to see society as divided into various potentially harmonious orders. Withal, they disliked demagogues and "popular leaders."[27] The Anti-Federalists were reluctant direct democrats precisely because they shied away from direct rule, in the Aristotelian sense, even by the many; they were attracted to direct democracy and indirect government at the same time. Still, they knew that the natural democrats outnumbered the natural aristocrats and that the farmers outnumbered everyone. And in the end the Anti-Federalists had few worries about the danger of *majority* faction, which Madison had identified in *Federalist* No. 10 as the effectual truth of "pure democracy." It was the few, the natural aristocrats, that the Anti-Federalists worried about.[28] Their typical prescription for the ills of republicanism was, therefore, to keep government "simple" and to make republican constitutions more populist or democratic. They favored a larger number of representatives, shorter terms of office, the right to recall congressmen, and term limits.

This tendency should not be exaggerated. The opponents of the Constitution believed in seeking the "best informed men" for office and so embraced, again reluctantly, the aristocratic principle of elections rather than the arch-democratic principle of selecting office-holders by lot.[29] But they had little faith in the outcome of elections. The Anti-Federalists preferred legislative dominance of politics because the legislators were closer or could be kept closer to the people than could executive officers, but they did not trust the legislators, either. In the end, they trusted, if anyone, only the elusive natural democrats.[30]

Instructing the Representatives

For our purposes, one of the most revealing side-debates in the founding period was over the issue of instructions, i.e., mandates to representatives from their constituents. Instructions were popular in America, particularly in Massachusetts, whose towns had been instructing their delegates to the General Court for more than a century (and where the people's right to instruct their representatives had been guaranteed in the 1780 constitution), but also in Pennsylvania, Virginia, and other states. Before and during the Revolution, these states had turned to mass meetings and grand-jury presentments in order to instruct their legislators about the Stamp Act and other outrages.[31] As an issue, instructions harked back to the Radical Whig critique of British parliamentary corruption. Parliament should not be a corrupt tool of the royal court, the Radicals had argued, but should reflect the interests of the Commons, and one way to accomplish this was to bind members of Parliament through mandates or instructions from their constituents. Instructions were a remarkably popular nostrum in America, and George Washington, John Adams, and even Alexander Hamilton supported them at one time or another at the state level.

In the first congress under the new Constitution, what would become the First Amendment occasioned an extensive debate over the propriety of instructions at the national level. It was moved that the words "to instruct their Representatives" be added to the rights protected under the amendment. Elbridge Gerry of Massachusetts commented that the friends of the Constitution (he had not been one of them) had always maintained that sovereignty resides with the people. But to say that "sovereignty vests in the people, and that they have not a right to instruct and control their representatives, is absurd to the last degree." Another congressman declared that "instruction and representation in a republic appear to me to be inseparably connected." But Roger Sherman of New York replied that if representatives "were to be guided by instructions, there would be no use in deliberation; all that a man would have to do, would be to produce his instructions, and lay them on the table, and let them speak for him." The right of the people "to consult for the common good" could therefore go no further than "to petition the legislature, or apply for a redress of grievances."

It was a good debate, spoiled perhaps only by the unwillingness of the two sides to be more unreasonable. Even Elbridge Gerry admitted, for example, that the proposed amendment would declare only "the right of the people to send instructions." What the representative would do with them, after communicating them to the House, would be up to him—he would have to "judge for himself."[32] The refusal to insist that instructions be binding reflected the reasonable way that instructions often had been interpreted in the states, too.[33] In any event, James Madison and his allies won the vote in the First Congress, and the right to instruct representatives was not added to the Constitution, though the issue would come up again in future congresses.

REPRESENTATION AND THE CONSTITUTION

Unlike the Anti-Federalists, Madison and other proponents of the Constitution looked at representation in a strongly favorable light. Although Madison never spelled out a complete theory of representation, and in *The Federalist* took pains to emphasize the varying qualities and characteristics expected of representation in the House and the Senate, he may be said to have supported a version of the independence theory. He deprecated the complete independence of representatives from their constituents, of course; a "dependence on the people" is essential to republicanism. But representatives must also be capable of exercising a "due responsibility" that goes beyond mere responsiveness to their constitutents' will.[34]

Other Federalists, particularly Noah Webster, went much further towards a pure theory of independence. Webster denied that elected office-holders are "servants of the people" or in any sense directly "accountable to them." The Constitution forbids legislators to be "called in question for their opinions or votes," he declared, and "the power of the people to omit choosing a representative at a subsequent election, is, by no means, a power to call him to account for his conduct."[35]

Madison never made such an argument, and in fact took pains in *The Federalist* to defend the House and Senate against the Anti-Federalists' charge that national legislators would be unaccountable to their constituents or states. For Madison, representation was a key part of the solution to the endemic problem of republican government, namely, its tendency to degenerate into one form or another of majority tyranny. Against the Anti-Federalist contention that the large size of the Union made representation unreliable and republicanism impossible, Madison argued that a large republic not only would reduce the chances of the formation of a majority faction but also would allow the principle of representation to have "its full effect." The Union's great size, which made representation necessary, would also make representation better and more effective, without sacrificing accountability. In fact, legislators in the House and Senate might be more accountable than state legislators, because the national legislators would be fewer, better known, and more clearly in the public eye.

In pressing his case in the famous *Federalist* No. 10, Madison distinguishes in a new way between a republic and a democracy. A "pure democracy"—probably the immediate antecedent of our term "direct democracy"—is "a society consisting of a small number of persons, who assemble and administer the government in person." Such a society "can admit of no cure for the mischiefs of faction," he says flatly, because "a common passion or interest will, in almost every case, be felt by a majority of the whole," and may be acted on rapidly. "Hence it is that such democracies have ever been spectacles of turbulence and contention; have ever been found incompatible with personal security or the rights of property; and have in general been as short in their lives as they have been violent in their deaths." Far from being the standard or ideal at which republicanism should aim, pure democracy is an inherently bad form of government. Madison goes out of his way to discredit it, to show that pure democracy is the perversion of popular government and that the friend of popular government must repair to a very different standard in order to vindicate his cause. By contrast, a republic, Madison writes, "is a government in which the scheme of representation takes place." A democracy cannot be a republic, and the republic is the only sound form of popular government."[36]

Representation: The Key to Good Government

Like Aristotle, Madison wishes to distinguish between healthy and unhealthy, defensible and indefensible forms of popular government; and like Aristotle, he terms the good form republican government and the bad, democracy. Whereas Aristotle located the crucial distinction between the two in the intentions of their rulers (the common good versus the selfish good of the many), Madison traces the difference to the presence or absence of representation. Representation becomes the key to good government or, more precisely, to the ability of popular government to become good government. The only question, then, is whether small or large republics conduce more to good government.

Madison decides this question in favor of large republics, mostly on the grounds that their greater size renders majority factions, the bane of popular governments, less likely. But as *The Federalist* proceeds, it becomes clear that perhaps the more important advantage of large republics is that they enable a more elaborate application of the principle of representation. The first effect of representation that he mentions, after all, is that it serves "to refine and enlarge the public views by passing them through the medium of a chosen body of citizens, whose wisdom may best discern the true interest of their country and whose patriotism and love of justice will be less likely to sacrifice it to temporary or partial considerations." And so we see the primary advantage of republican over democratic government: "Under such a regulation it may well happen that the public voice, pronounced by the representatives of the people, will be more consonant to the public good than if pronounced by the people themselves, convened for the purpose."[37]

Whereas for the opponents of the Constitution, representation is a kind of necessary evil, for defenders of the Constitution it is a positive good, and in the later pages of *The Federalist* Madison and Hamilton explain the obvious and the subtle ways in which representation will work its good on the House, the Senate, and the executive. In general, "Publius" argues that the characteristics of each branch—its organization, powers, duration, and number of officeholders—will elicit "fit characters" to perform the required duties. In other words, the representative principle assumes a different aspect in each branch, depending on the nature of its powers and duties. To be sure, "the effect may be inverted" and unfit characters elected to office, but their depredations will be limited—and, conversely, the beneficial deeds of good office-holders will be enhanced—by the Constitution's artful separation of powers.[38] Because the branches are able to check one another, it is safe to make them robust, and "Publius" defends as essential to republicanism those features that the Anti-Federalists feared as antithetical to republicanism: no annual elections and a small number of representatives in the House, a long term of office and considerable power in the small Senate, a unitary executive with no term limits, a federal bench of unelected judges with good-behavior tenure.

"Total Exclusion of the People . . ."

The flip side of the separation of powers is that it encourages each branch to perform its peculiar functions well. Combining liberty with stability and energy, the House, the Senate, and the presidency form a government that is able to deliberate and act responsibly. Unlike the situation in direct democracy, deliberation under the republican Constitution takes place primarily among the officeholders, not among the citizens, though there is an extended and important sense in which the citizens, in elections, are called upon to deliberate on the overall course of government. Still, a distinctive feature of our republicanism is what Madison candidly and emphatically calls "*the total exclusion of the people in their collective capacity*" from any share in administering the government.[39] In direct democracy, the people, so to speak, *are* the government. Under the Constitution, the people have no part in running the government at all; the work is done by the elected and appointed officials of the three branches. But as a result, the government as a whole is made responsible to and for the people, who are the source of its legitimacy and the judge of its officers. Paradoxically, leaving the administration of government to constitutional officeholders confirms rather than dilutes the people's sovereignty.[40]

At the same time that their government is rendered more responsible it is also made more rational. In Madison's language, "it is the reason, alone, of the public, that ought to control and regulate the government. The passions ought to be controlled and regulated by the government." The Constitution, embodying not tyrannical reason but "the reason of the public," presides over the government, keeping it to a rational yet popular course. The judiciary serves to remind the other branches and the people of the majesty and reasonableness of the law that Americans live under and are obliged to live up to. The people's own views are "refined and enlarged" into a kind of reverence for the law—an example of passion allying with reason so that passion does not have to be "controlled and regulated" so much by the government.

In short, a rational Constitution helps to shape a reasonable public opinion, which may then "control and regulate" the government, through elections, in the spirit of the Constitution. Neither the people nor the government can ever be perfectly rational, of course, but a good Constitution fosters "the cool and deliberate sense of the community." It is this sense—not direct democracy's weakness for popular whims and sentiments, nor, for that matter, Progressivism's foolish confidence that popular will is ultimately rational will—that Madison seeks to cultivate through republican constitutionalism. But he emphasizes soberly that this sense will break down occasionally, and that only the "interference of some temperate and respectable body of citizens" or men of considerable "courage and magnanimity" may save the people from their own folly.[41]

In their advocacy of the initiative, referendum, and other devices of direct democracy, the Progressives made much of the development in the founding period of popular ratification of constitutions, whether by plebiscites (in town meetings) or by conventions. Madison, too, was keen to have the new Constitution ratified not by the state legislatures but by special state ratifying conventions, in order to baptize it in the pure waters of popular authority. But the Progressives regarded the Founders' solicitude for popular ratification as a precedent that could be used to press for a greater popular role in ordinary lawmaking.

On this, the Progressives got it exactly wrong. Madison's point was that such "experiments are of too ticklish a nature to be unnecessarily multiplied." If the people were constantly involved in making or reviewing laws, they would soon lose respect for the law. Popular passions and the spirit of pre-existing or emergent parties would substitute for reflection on "the true merits of the question." Once the distinction between fundamental law, ratified by the people, and statute law, passed by their representatives, collapsed, popular government under the rule of law would itself be imperiled.[42] That experiments in direct democracy at the state level have proved more or less tolerable, and occasionally even useful, should not lead us to undervalue what the Founders bequeathed to us: the constitutional framework that keeps the costs of such experiments low.

CHAPTER TWO

James Madison and the Spirit of 1787

Gary Rosen

In today's debate over direct democracy, it is hard to escape the vener-able phrase "We the People," and for good reason. As the advocates of initiative, referendum, and other plebiscitary practices appreciate, the idea of popular sovereignty, so neatly encapsulated in these proud opening words of the U.S. Constitution, still very much resonates with Americans. After all, what principle in our political tradition is more firmly estab-lished than the ultimate right of the people to take questions of policy and constitutional structure into their own hands, doing for themselves what their representatives are unwilling or unable to do for them?

There is no disputing the distinguished historical pedigree—or rhe-torical power—of this view, but it is instructive, especially in trying to shed some light on present-day concerns, to see where the idea of popular sovereignty came from and how it was understood by those most re-sponsible for introducing it into American political thought. As far as the Constitution itself is concerned, the inescapable authority on this matter is James Madison, the most influential member of the Federal Convention of 1787 and co-author of *The Federalist*, the classic defense of that gathering's handiwork. For his part, Madison often pointed to a still earlier source as the foremost expression in America of the idea of

Gary Rosen is the managing editor of *Commentary* and the author of *American Compact: James Madison and the Problem of Founding* (1999). His articles and reviews have appeared in *Commentary*, the *Wall Street Journal*, *First Things*, *The Review of Politics*, the *American Journal of Ju-risprudence*, and other publications.

19

popular sovereignty: the Declaration of Independence, written by his great friend and political ally Thomas Jefferson.

For all Madison's deference to Jefferson, however, the two Virginians disagreed rather sharply about the precise nature and extent of this most fundamental form of popular authority. Put more philosophically, their disagreement stemmed from the rather different conclusions they drew from the social compact, the root idea not only of their own political thought but of the American Revolution more generally. If Jefferson was the purest representative of the Spirit of 1776—that is, of the radically democratic claims of the Declaration of Independence—Madison embodied a rival interpretation of the social compact, one that emerged from the actual making of the Constitution a little more than a decade later. It is this spirit, I would suggest, the Spirit of 1787, from which we have the most to learn today.

The Radicalism of the Social Compact

In the modern political world, the social compact is a familiar idea, an almost intuitive explanation for what makes governments legitimate. This familiarity often keeps us from recognizing just how radical the social compact was when the idea was first introduced in the seventeenth century, in the writings of the political philosophers Thomas Hobbes and John Locke. If for most of human history government was based on claims about God's will or the privileges of a particular class—or, more generally, just on a tradition of some sort—under the social compact government was seen for the first time as the *creation* of the people as a whole; it was an instrument that they wielded to protect themselves and their most fundamental interests, or what Locke summarized as "life, liberty, and estate."

In America, the best-known formulation of this idea can be found, of course, in the Declaration of Independence. As Jefferson wrote, with unmistakable allusions to Locke,

> We hold these truths to be self-evident, that all Men are created equal, that they are endowed by their Creator with certain unalienable Rights, that among these are Life, Liberty, and the Pursuit of Happiness—That to secure these Rights, Governments are instituted among Men, deriving their just Powers from the Consent of the Governed, that whenever any Form of Government becomes destructive of these Ends, it is the Right of the People to

alter or to abolish it, and to institute new Government, laying its Foundation on such Principles, and organizing its Powers in such Form, as to them shall seem most likely to effect their Safety and Happiness.

This is very bold stuff, especially when considered in the context of its day. What it involves, above all, is a profound notion of human equality. It gives to everyone—to every member of society, in principle—a say in what the basic structure of government should look like. The original purpose of the idea, particularly in the writings of Locke, was to keep existing political institutions in line, to remind kings and aristocrats that they ignored the common weal—the rights and interests of the general public—at their own peril. The message was simple: Serve the people, or the people will replace you with rulers who will. In Locke, this finds expression as the "right of revolution," but one can also think of it, less dramatically, as the looming threat of direct democracy.

In embracing this idea, however, the American founders quickly realized that their situation was quite different from that of seventeenth-century England. Rather than needing to keep old institutions in line, the newly independent Americans needed to start from scratch, to build entirely new political institutions. But here was the rub. While it may have been "self-evident" that they had the *right* to make new governments, it was far from self-evident just how they were to go about doing it. Who, exactly, was supposed to do the constitution-making?

Diversity in the Service of Unity

It is with this problem that James Madison. one of the youngest members of the founding generation, enters the picture Still a budding revolutionary when Jefferson was writing the Declaration of Independence, Madison first appeared on the national scene in 1780, when at the age of 29 he joined the Virginia delegation in the Continental Congress. Within a year of his arrival, the states had ratified the first—and now only dimly remembered—American constitution, the Articles of Confederation.

The Confederation was a hopelessly ineffective national government, largely because its organizing principle was to treat all the states equally, almost as fully independent nations. Each had just one vote in the Continental Congress, and unanimity was required for any change in the Articles themselves. As a result, state legislatures frequently ignored the authority of Congress, and nowhere more so than in its requisitions for funds. For three years Madison worked tirelessly to reform the Confederation, especially to win for it an independent source of revenue. But his proposals were rejected one after another, usually the victim of the Articles' requirement of unanimity.

Late in 1783, having completed his term as a delegate (and, despite his youth, having quickly won a national reputation), Madison returned to Virginia, deeply troubled by the worsening national situation. How, he wondered, would it be possible to make a more effective national government? Any new government would have to be ratified by the people. But could the plan for a new government come *from* the people? Could they be counted on to know what the nation needed and what institutions were required to achieve it?

Madison was doubtful. He had seen the profound difficulties involved in adding a few modest powers to the Articles of Confederation. The people, he believed, were too attached to the sovereign claims of their state governments and too easily swayed by their own varied and often conflicting interests. A few years later, in *Federalist* 10, he would describe the multitudinous groups representing these narrow views as "factions," and he would blame them for the political instability and indifference to minority rights that were so common throughout the country at the time.

But that was not the end of the matter for Madison. The fame of *Federalist* 10 rests on his counterintuitive insight that, for all the difficulties posed by the country's countless parties, interests, and sects, such social diversity could be an instrument of national unity and good government when brought together in one "extended sphere," that is, under the Constitution. Such a regime, he wrote, would make it "less probable that a majority of the whole will have a common motive to invade the rights of other citizens; or if such a common motive exists, it will be more difficult for all who feel it to discover their own strength, and to act in unison with each other."

What is too often overlooked in interpretations of *Federalist* 10, however, is the extent to which Madison's argument about the salutary effects of diversity points to a prior, more practical question: how was such a welter of parties, interests, and sects to be brought into a single national government in the first place? Surely the very problems that called for an extended sphere would make popular assent to its establishment unlikely; factious sorts would have to be willing to participate in a regime whose avowed purpose was to thwart them. Madison spoke of this problem in *Federalist* 37, and with obvious reference to Number 10. "Although this variety of interests, for reasons sufficiently explained in a former paper, may have a salutary influence on the administration of the government *when formed*," he wrote, "every one must be sensible of the contrary influence which must have been experienced *in the task of forming it*" (emphasis added).

Constitutional Conventions

The remedy that Madison eventually hit upon was the calling of a constitutional convention. Today we tend to view constitutional conventions as very matter-of-fact things, but they were a profound political innovation—and an American one at that. They fill an obvious need in the theory of the social compact. After all, you cannot literally bring all the people together to make a government; from a strictly administrative point of view, that would be wildly impractical. Constitutional conventions provided an alternative: a gathering of representatives specially empowered to express the people's will for them.

Like many other American statesmen of the day, Madison recognized these advantages, but he also came to see conventions as far more than a convenient substitute for the people as a whole. To his mind, they also provided an opportunity to *circumvent* the people, even if just temporarily. Indeed, he eventually concluded that constitutional conventions were a necessary device for allowing those like himself—"the most enlightened and influential patriots," as he put it—to escape from popular institutions so that they could put popular government on a sounder and more permanent footing.

In this regard, it is important to remember the somewhat irregular circumstances surrounding the Federal Convention of 1787. It was not the states themselves or the Continental Congress that issued the original request for delegates to meet in Philadelphia. Rather, the call came forth from a small gathering that took place in 1786 and was known as the Annapolis Convention. This meeting was supposed to be confined to recommending better ways for regulating commerce, but Madison, Alexander Hamilton, and the other notables who attended decided to do more. As Madison later wrote, they "did not scruple to decline the limited task assigned to [them]." Instead of addressing the narrow question of commercial regulation, they called upon the states to send fully empowered delegates to a grander convention. This next, much more famous convention took place in Philadelphia in the summer of 1787.

We often forget that the Federal Convention of 1787, like the Annapolis Convention before it, was assigned a limited purpose, and that the Constitution it produced was an unwelcome surprise to much of the nation. The delegates had been asked to figure out a way to strengthen the union, and it was assumed that they would preserve the basic form of the Articles of Confederation—that is, the principle that all the states were perfectly equal, and that each would have just one vote in deciding national policy. But such a regime was never really in the cards at Philadelphia.

In the end, the delegates to the Federal Convention did not even pretend to be amending the Articles. They promulgated a brand-new Constitution and asked that it be ratified not by the state legislatures, as the Articles required, but by the people themselves. Most scandalous of all, they proclaimed that the approval of just nine states, instead of the unanimity required by the Articles, would suffice to ratify the new Constitution. Two centuries later, we can no longer fully appreciate just how outrageous an assumption of authority this was, but many Americans were understandably indignant at the time. As they saw it, a duly established national government had been discarded without a second thought.

Restricting Popular Sovereignty

In the debate in Philadelphia over whether the delegates should respect the limits imposed on them by the Confederation and the state governments, Madison did not mince words:

> We ought to consider what [is] right & necessary in itself for the attainment of a proper Government. A plan adjusted to this idea will recommend itself. . . . All the most enlightened and respectable citizens will be its advocates. Should we fall short of the necessary and proper point, this influential class of citizens will be turned against the plan, and little support in opposition to them can be gained to it from the unreflecting multitude.

Madison was uninterested, in short, not only in the formal instructions that had been given to the delegates, but also in the immediate views of the American people themselves. This "unreflecting multitude" would simply follow the opinions of the country's leading men.

Madison did not change his mind in the wake of the Federal Convention. While the ratification debate was going on in 1788, he received a letter from his fellow Virginian Edmund Randolph, who had refused to sign the Constitution as a delegate in Philadelphia. Randolph was sympathetic to the calls then being heard for a second constitutional convention, one that would be more open about its aims and more fully informed by popular opinion. Madison would have none of it, and did not hesitate to repeat his candid view of the people's limits:

> Whatever respect may be due to the rights of private judgment, and no man feels more of it than I do, there can be no doubt that there are subjects to which the bulk of mankind are unequal, and on which they must and will be governed by those with whom they happen to have acquaintance and confidence. The proposed Constitution is of this description.

I do not mean to paint Madison as some kind of anti-republican ogre. Throughout his long career he was a firm and principled believer in the cause of popular government. Indeed, just a week after sharing his impolitic views with Edmund Randolph, he published *Federalist 39*, where he proudly insisted that the new Constitution was "strictly republican," that is, that its day-to-day operations would reflect the will of the people. "It is evident," he wrote, "that no other form would be reconcileable with the genius of the people of America; with the fundamental principles of the revolution; or with that honorable determination, which animates every votary of freedom, to rest all our political experiments on the capacity of mankind for self-government."

There is no reason to consider this statement any less sincere than Madison's somewhat shocking remarks to the members of the Federal Convention and to Randolph, or to think that he saw himself as anything but a "votary of freedom." But what Madison understood is that the Declaration of Independence, like the social-compact theory on which it was based, needed some amending. The people, it turned out, required a good deal of help in creating a constitution that would be adequate to their needs. As he saw it, the essential lesson of 1787 was that popular sovereignty had to be limited if it was not to destroy the possibility of stable, moderate self-government.*

---

* This effort to "amend" the Declaration of Independence was not merely figurative. In *Federalist* 40, while defending the latitude assumed by the Federal Convention, Madison quoted the Declaration for support—but his excerpt contained a telling omission, included here in brackets. It was the right of the

Jefferson's Alternative

Madison's chastened view of popular sovereignty was hardly universal among the members of the founding generation. As I suggested at the outset, his great friend and political ally Thomas Jefferson saw no need to qualify the version of the social compact that he had described so eloquently in the Declaration of Independence. If the people were the true source of all just political authority, Jefferson reasoned, and if government was the instrument by which they achieved their ends, there should be some regular opportunity for them to review their political institutions, free from the obstacles of everyday politics and the influence of their often corrupt representatives.

As a practical matter, this led Jefferson to propose a number of schemes in the course of his career under which the people could reconsider not just particular policies but the very form of their government. The most radical of these proposals is contained in a famous letter that Jefferson wrote to Madison in the closing months of 1789, as Jefferson was preparing to return to the United States after four years as ambassador to France. With the early events of the French Revolution fresh in his mind, Jefferson asked, "whether one generation of men has a right to bind another." His answer was a resounding no: "no such obligation can be so transmitted." In fact, Jefferson concluded that all public measures, including constitutions, naturally expired with the passing of the generation responsible for them, a period of some nineteen years by his own actuarial calculations. Thus the Constitution that Madison and the others had just labored with such difficulty to establish would lose all legitimacy, he suggested, by 1808. "If it be enforced longer," he wrote, "it is an act of force, and not of right." Nor, Jefferson hastened to add, was the hypothetical possibility of repeal or the existence of popular self-government an adequate substitute. However well contrived a form of government, it inevitably created impediments to the expression of the true "will of the majority." The only way to ensure that constitutions and laws were not an imposition—an "act of force"—was to require the people to start anew at some regular interval.

---

people, he wrote, to "abolish or alter their governments [and to institute new Government, laying its Foundation on such Principles, and organizing its Powers in such Form] as to them shall seem most likely to effect their Safety and Happiness." Madison's abridgement, unnoted in the text, represents a subtle but unmistakable challenge to the prudential claims of the people.

Popular sovereignty also formed the theoretical backdrop of Jefferson's various proposals over the years for maintaining the limits and boundaries of established constitutions. In his *Notes on the State of Virginia* (1787), for example, he argued that disputes over the separation of powers should not be left to officeholders themselves to decide or resolve. Rather, in keeping with the Spirit of 1776, such "breaches" should be "corrected," he believed, by the sovereign people, acting through specially chosen conventions.

Later, in his well-known Kentucky Resolutions, Jefferson again resorted to first principles, this time against the Congress and President who had seen fit to pass the Alien and Sedition Acts of 1798. If the federal government was going to pass such plainly unconstitutional measures, he argued, the states, as original parties to the social compact, possessed a "natural right" to declare these acts "void and of no force." Indeed, as Jefferson had written in an early draft of the resolutions, "every state has a natural right in cases not within the compact . . . to nullify of their own authority all assumptions of power by others within their limits"—a line of reasoning eventually adopted by John C. Calhoun and his followers in advocating the cause of nullification.

A final instance of Jefferson's faith in popular sovereignty can be seen in his response, toward the end of his life, to the most controversial rulings of the Supreme Court under Chief Justice John Marshall. Outraged by the decisions in the landmark cases *McCulloch v. Maryland* (1819) and *Cohens v. Virginia* (1821), Jefferson concluded that Marshall was bent on giving unlimited powers to the national government, thereby completing the assault on the Constitution launched by Hamilton in the 1790s. His remedy for such overreaching was familiar. The authority to resolve disputes between the federal government and the states should be taken away from the Supreme Court, he told his correspondents, and placed in the safe hands of the sovereign people, acting, once more, through conventions. The popular will would take the place of judicial review.

Madison's Reply

In all these cases Madison made roughly the same reply to his friend and fellow Virginian. First, of course, he was quick to congratulate Jefferson on his brilliance and sound general principles. "Like everything from the same pen," Madison observed in *Federalist* 49, the constitutional scheme described in Jefferson's *Notes* "marks a turn of thinking original, comprehensive, and accurate; and is the more worthy of attention, as it equally displays a fervent attachment to republican government, and an enlightened view of the dangerous propensities against which it ought to be guarded."

With the substance of Jefferson's proposals Madison was less forgiving. There was, to begin with, the question of practicality. As he gently suggested in response to Jefferson's letter from France, a prohibition on laws with a term of more than nineteen years would prevent the present generation from making necessary exertions "for the benefit of posterity," like paying off the national debt. Moreover, if ordinary laws lapsed at stated times, "violent struggles" would ensue over the fundamentals of property relations, leading at best to an arbitrariness incompatible with "steady industry" and at worst to anarchy. Nor were the practical difficulties any less severe with regard to Jefferson's favorite mechanism for consulting the popular sovereign. "To refer every point of disagreement [over the Constitution] to the people in Conventions," Madison objected to Jefferson in an 1823 letter, "would be a process too tardy, too troublesome, and too expensive."

But Madison's most serious response to Jefferson's schemes was that the Constitution itself simply could not withstand such regular recourse to the sovereign authority of the people. If the Constitution was to last—and to keep republicanism from degenerating into majority capriciousness or oppression—it would have to stand at some distance from the immediate wishes of the people, retaining "that share of prejudice in its favor which is a salutary aid to the most rational government." As he wrote in *Federalist* 49, in a reply to Jefferson worth quoting at length,

As every appeal to the people would carry an implication of some defect in the government, frequent appeals would in great measure deprive the government of that veneration, which time bestows on everything, and without which perhaps the wisest and freest governments would not possess the requisite stability. If it be true that all governments rest on opinion, it is no less true that the strength of opinion in each individual, and its practical influence on his conduct, depend much on the number which he supposes to have entertained the same opinion. The reason of man, like man himself is timid and cautious, when left alone; and acquires firmness and confidence, in proportion to the number with which it is associated. When the examples, which fortify opinion, are *ancient* as well as *numerous*, they are known to have a double effect. In a nation of philosophers, this consideration ought to be disregarded. A reverence for the laws, would be sufficiently inculcated by the voice of an enlightened reason. But a nation of philosophers is as little to be expected as the philosophical race of kings wished for by Plato. And in every other nation, the most rational government will not find it a superfluous advantage, to have the prejudices of the community on its side.

The almost pietistic terms used by Madison in these passages—"prejudice," "veneration," "reverence"—have been seen by some modern commentators as recommending an attitude of quiet respect, if not outright submission, on the part of the people. Madison's tone is unmistakably that of a traditionalist, of someone anxious to preserve established institutions. But it is important not to exaggerate how far he goes here in rejecting the claims and capacities of the people. In a regime based explicitly on the people's transhistorical right to alter or abolish constitutions, Madison suggests, the fact that previous generations have not felt the need to avail themselves of this right should carry some weight.

In this light, the past can be seen as an extended referendum on constitutional arrangements. "Ancient" examples fortify opinion, not because they represent the superior wisdom or inspiration of founders, but because they multiply the number of people who have held that opinion. For Madison, constitutional "veneration" was not meant to be a wholly irrational attachment. Rather, it would be a consequence of constitutional success over time, insulating the regime from precipitous change but not from all critical scrutiny. Thus it was only a "salutary aid," a "not . . . superfluous advantage." The performance of a regime, its "rationality" in terms of its declared ends, was what ultimately decided its fate under the social compact.

More to the point perhaps, and as Madison emphasized throughout *The Federalist*, the essential prerogatives of the people were already firmly enshrined in the Constitution. Madison did not subscribe to Jefferson's dire pronouncements about the inevitable corruption of the public councils and the impossibility of designing a form of government that would reliably reflect the will of the majority. A "well constituted" government, as he called it, could provide for a proper institutional dependence of its officers on the people and, failing that, for an orderly process of amendment on those "great and extraordinary occasions" when it was warranted.

Given such formal arrangements, a spirited people, taught to regard government as their own creation, would be vigilant enough to see that their rights and interests were attended to. As Madison declared in exasperation to his Anti-Federalist critics (and by extension to Jefferson), "What are we to say to the men who profess the most flaming zeal for Republican Government yet boldly impeach the fundamental principle of it; who pretend to be champions of the right and the capacity of the people to choose their own rulers, yet maintain that they will prefer those only who will immediately and infallibly betray the trust committed to them?" This was the paradox at the heart of Anti-Federalist thought, and it applied with special force to Jefferson's most radical proposals. If, as he suggested, the people lacked the character and intellect necessary for *maintaining* a republican constitution, how could they be expected to model their constitutions anew in every generation?

Madison expected the people to exert their rightful influence, but he wanted them to do so through their elected representatives, and in the last resort, through the amendment power set out in the Constitution itself. What he feared, and saw as antithetical to the Spirit of 1787, was any effort to reproduce in all its breadth the awesome popular authority—the *sovereign* authority—described by the social compact. The people were indeed the best overseers of their own rights and interests, but only when they acted through the forms of the Constitution. If they acted directly, Madison believed, the result would be the same instability and injustice that had made it necessary to establish a new constitution in the first place.

Poll-Driven Politics

Where does all this leave us today, with our tracking polls and focus groups, with Ron Unz and Ward Connerly and Dick Morris, and with more initiatives and referendums than anyone can count? Those who favor a greater direct role for the people tend, for obvious reasons, to be great fans of Jefferson, and they make the same compelling argument that he did almost two centuries ago: that only the people, acting as sovereign, can be relied on to correct certain kinds of corruption or unresponsiveness in government.

What's more, they say, Madison's objections to popular authority were overdrawn and elitist even in his own day and are especially out of place now. After all, the Constitution is hardly in danger of dissolving at this late date, and the three branches of government are, if anything, too secure in their habits and prerogatives—and in their cozy relationship with bureaucrats and interest groups. Nor are the initiatives and referendums that are today's most obvious instances of direct democracy even aimed at the federal government. They operate instead at the state level, serving much the same function as federalism by encouraging experimentation and broadening the national debate on controversial issues. Now more than ever before, we are told, the Spirit of 1776 is a safe and necessary corrective to the failings of representative government.

There is certainly something to be said for these arguments, and it is difficult not to think of measures like Proposition 209 and Proposition 227—the California ballot initiatives that overturned, respectively, affirmative action and bilingual education—as significant advances. But I do worry, and my worries are Madisonian.

In the first place, we should not exaggerate the degree to which direct democracy has resulted in better policies at the state level or a more enlightened national debate. For every Proposition 209, there is, unfortunately, something like the anti-immigrant Proposition 187, which not only was a bad idea in itself but needlessly inflamed ethnic passions in California and elsewhere. Similar damage may be done in the long run by the unsuccessful initiative on the 2000 ballot in California that would have "voucherized" the state's entire public-school system—a premature and grossly impolitic proposal whose defeat was foreseen by more sober advocates of school choice. For all the genuine benefits that have arisen from initiative and referendum, in short, recent history does little to contradict Madison's concerns about the parochialism of state politics and the dangers of direct popular action.

More broadly, I fear that in our rush to create ever more avenues for the direct expression of the popular will, we too often take the Constitution itself for granted and forget that maintaining it requires certain political attitudes and dispositions, what Madison called "veneration." As I see it, the constitutional forms that have guided and defined our politics—and shaped our character as a constitutional people—are very much at risk today.

This is not just because many Americans are fed up with politicians, or because we do a lousy job teaching our children the reasoning and history behind the Constitution. Rather, I think that the very idea of constitutionalism is increasingly viewed with suspicion, in large part because the potential for genuine mass democracy—for the direct participation of the people in the key decisions of government—is greater today than ever before, and promises only to grow.

The American people have come to see politics as an endless string of opinion polls, with the final one on election day having lost not only its drama but much of its meaning as well. They are also well disposed to the idea of initiative and referendum, even in states where it is not currently available. Their expectation, increasingly, is that the views of their leaders will be an immediate reflection of their own. Indeed, it is not difficult to imagine a time, a few years down the road, when there will be a demand for technology that will allow citizens to make their opinions regularly known, and perhaps even to vote, from the comfort of their homes. Nor is it difficult to imagine politicians who will gladly endorse such electronic plebiscites.

One way to head off this possibility is for our political leaders to do a better job of setting an agenda and trying to persuade the public of its soundness, instead of just manufacturing a new policy in response to every blip in the opinion polls. But some rethinking may be order as well for the activists and advocates who are today so busily trying to bring into their corner the mighty weight of the popular sovereign. My suggestion to them is straightforward: rather than turning directly to the people when we cannot get politicians to do what needs to be done, perhaps we should work harder to elect a new batch of politicians.

Such advice is unlikely to satisfy those who are impatient for political change and who long for decisive and immediate victories. But following it would make some small difference, I believe, in resisting the contemporary tide against the institutions and principles of representative government—and would pay due respect to the wisdom of James Madison and the Spirit of 1787.

CHAPTER THREE

Lincoln's View of Direct Democracy and Public Opinion

Herman Belz

In a speech at Edwardsville, Illinois, in 1858, in the midst of the Lincoln-Douglas debates, Abraham Lincoln stated: "The idea of Popular Sovereignty was floating about the world . . . before Columbus set foot on the American continent." Lincoln was right, and what he said aptly described the way writers on politics since ancient times had speculated on the part to be played by the people in a well-ordered regime. Popular self-government, he observed, "took tangible form" in 1776 in the "noble words" of the Declaration of Independence: "'We hold these truths to be self-evident: That all men are created equal; That they are endowed by their Creator with certain inalienable rights; . . . That to secure these rights governments are instituted among men, *deriving their just powers from the consent of the governed.*'" "If that is not Popular Sovereignty," said Lincoln, "then I have no conception of the meaning of words."[1]

Despite animadversions from both the egalitarian left and the libertarian right, Abraham Lincoln's stature as the preeminent authority on representative self-government in the American political tradition re-

Herman Belz is professor of history at the University of Maryland, College Park. His books include *The Webster-Hayne Debate on the Nature of the Union: Selected Documents* (2000), *A Living Constitution or Fundamental Law?* (1998), and *Abraham Lincoln, Constitutionalism, and Equal Rights in the Civil War Era* (1998).

33

mains secure. Moreover, the essential problems of democratic theory that he faced in the Civil War era persist in American politics. In the climate of multiculturalism there is renewed controversy about the identity of "the governed" whose consent confers legitimacy on government. How are the people constituted? By what forms and procedures are they to be represented in government, their consent given, their opinion on specific issues made known? Perhaps the foremost problem in democratic theory today is the tendency of contemporary populists and students of public opinion to regard the people as a law unto themselves, unlimited by any other source of authority natural or divine. Lincoln did not make this mistake. For this reason above all, his views on the nature and tendencies of representative government based on public opinion provide insight into enduring issues in American constitutionalism.

While debate persists over whether Lincoln preserved or destroyed the Founders' Constitution, something close to willful disregard of the historical record is required to deny his oft-expressed fidelity to the design and intent of the Constitution. Although his speeches and letters do not cite *The Federalist*, Lincoln agreed with James Madison that the distinctive advantage of American representation is the total exclusion of the people "in their collective capacity" from government. Affirming the priority of reason over passion as an influence on political life, Lincoln further concurred in the belief that too frequent recourse to the people on matters of constitutional structure is unwise; yet he also said that even the most rational government will find it an advantage to have "the prejudices of the community on its side."

Lincoln believed the will of the people could be identified through constitutionally prescribed forms of representation, and expressed in legislative deliberation and decision. The will of the people as communicated in public opinion imposed moral and constitutional obligation on government officials. Lincoln held that the legislative branch, rather than the executive, was the institution through which the popular will should manifest itself. At the same time he recognized limits on the role of public opinion. While the will of the people ought to determine the basic direction of public policy, public opinion ought not to control—because as a practical matter it *could not* control—the administration of government. Lincoln's executive statesmanship rested on the conviction that public opinion did not obviate or overrule the prudential and constitutional judgments required of government officials by the contingent nature of political life.

Lincoln resisted the tendency, perhaps inevitable in representative democracy, to take unstructured public opinion as the collective will of the people. He viewed institutions of representation and opinion formation as means by which legitimate authority is transmitted to government officials. Lincoln rejected, in other words, the idea that in representative democracy the people retain sovereign governing power and can give orders to government officials, who lack genuine authority.[2]

Two Views of Public Opinion

What do we mean and what did Lincoln mean by the term "public opinion"? The phenomenon of public opinion developed in early modern history with the emergence of the public sphere and the idea of publicity. Since the eighteenth century, two fundamentally different conceptions have been advanced. The first regards public opinion as a unified, objective, substantive thing, embodied in knowable principles and ideas that have universal validity. Public opinion is seen as a kind of political or social actor. The second and more recent conception defines public opinion in pluralistic, subjective terms. It is seen as a product of culturally contextualized views appearing throughout a particular society. Public opinion is therefore considered ephemeral, unstable, and relative, though subject to quantification and aggregation that may give the illusion of objective rationality.[3]

Public opinion in the first of these two senses was a feature of the emergence of democratic political theory in the eighteenth century, signifying the transition from absolute government to the rule of law and the rise of universal legal norms. The concept was integral to a system of public authority in which the consent of the governed was needed to legitimize laws and policies. Public opinion was associated with representative government, majority rule, and the people's sovereignty.

Lincoln viewed public opinion primarily in this first sense, in which it embodies universal, objective, rational principles and ideas. This can be seen in those well-known references in his speeches to the "universal sense of mankind," "public sentiment," and "a universal feeling" as enduring elements of political community and government. Yet Lincoln was actively involved in partisan politics in an increasingly pluralistic society, and he also recognized that public opinion could have a more particularistic and relative meaning, in which rationality is reduced to the subjective views of the individuals who constitute the public.[4]

Although both in time and in political temperament Lincoln was not far removed from the founding generation, the cultural environment of politics had changed significantly by his day. Improved means of communication made public opinion a more potent force. Print culture made possible the creation of a public sphere in which an aggressively democratic political system superseded the deferential political order of the eighteenth century. Permanent, ideologically coherent political parties formed, cultivating mass constituencies and transmitting the opinions of the people to the institutions of government. Voluntary associations appealed for citizen support on a wide variety of political, social, and religious causes, seeking through mass petition campaigns to influence opinions in society and government. By 1850 the country had two thousand newspapers, two hundred of them dailies. Closely aligned with political parties, an energetic free press both reported political opinion and actively shaped it.[5]

Lincoln was keenly aware of print culture and its significance. In a lecture on discoveries and inventions in 1859, describing the development of written material, he said:

> At length printing came. It gave ten thousand copies of any written matter, quite as cheaply as ten were given before; and consequently a thousand minds were brought into the field where there was but one before. This was a great gain. . . . I will venture to consider *it*, the true termination of that period called "the dark ages." [6]

In April 1865, Lincoln told a crowd gathered to celebrate the end of the war that at that moment he was "not ready to say anything that one in my position ought to say." He explained his hesitation: "Everything I say, you know, goes into print. If I make a mistake it doesn't merely affect me nor you but the country."[7] Lincoln realized that the phenomenon of mass communications had the potential to change the relationship between the people and their government. In far more compelling ways than in the founding era, the question was raised whether it was the duty of elected lawmakers and executive officers to carry out the will of the people as expressed in public opinion, or to filter and refine popular views in the light of an obligation to exercise authority according to their own ideas of moral and constitutional responsibility.

The changing environment of American politics had theoretical implications. Where representative institutions are subject to egalitarian pressures, the distinction between direct and indirect democracy blurs.

In a formal institutional sense the people may not assemble as a collective whole, directly exercising the power of government themselves. But if it is true that the idea of unmediated popular rule in a deep sense informs every type of representative government, and that, as the philosopher Yves Simon observed, "every democracy remains, in varying degree, a direct democracy," then the possibility exists that representative government will be corrupted into the rule of public opinion. The will of the people can, in Bertrand de Jouvenel's words, be abstracted into "the magic formula, popular sovereignty," divorced from any actual representative and deliberative assembly. The not unlikely result is the disintegration of genuine authority and responsible government.[8]

I believe that the possibility of creating this type of direct democracy existed in the nineteenth century, and that Lincoln's statesmanship was distinguished by resistance to it.

LINCOLN AND POPULAR SOVEREIGNTY

Lincoln's public life was dominated by confrontation with Democratic-party popular sovereignty, first in the controversy over the extension of slavery into the territories, and then in the secession crisis. His preparation for this work came from years of experience in Illinois politics as a member of the Whig party, whose primary reason for existence was to limit the claims of President Andrew Jackson to executive authority. Advocating election of the president by the people without regard to state lines, Jackson's Democratic party aimed to establish a more directly democratic form of popular sovereignty. In the opinion of the Whig opposition, this purpose threatened to subvert the republican government of the founding.

Early in his career Lincoln indicated the main themes of the political project that would define his achievement as a democratic statesman. In an address to the Springfield Lyceum in 1838, he reflected on the task of protecting the "political edifice of liberty and equal rights" established by the revolutionary fathers from the danger of direct democracy. The violent action of lawless mobs, such as the hanging of gamblers in Mississippi and the burning of mulattoes in Missouri, presented the immediate threat. Should the mobocratic spirit spread throughout the country, Lincoln warned, legal guarantees for the protection of person and property would be disregarded and "the *attachment* of the People," the strongest bulwark of any government, destroyed. Men of talent and ambition would seize the opportunity, strike the blow, and "subvert our national freedom." To meet the danger Lincoln recommended that reverence for the Constitution and the laws "become the *political religion* of the nation."[9]

In the "Temperance Address" of 1842 Lincoln offered a more considered argument for preserving civil and religious liberty. Instead of simply appealing to obedience to the Constitution and the laws, he took into account the positive use to be made of the right of revolutionary resistance on which the country was founded. "Of our political revolution of '76, we are all justly proud," Lincoln said. The Revolution gave Americans political freedom exceeding that of all other nations on earth. "In it," Lincoln asserted, "the world has found a solution of that long mooted problem, as to the capability of man to govern himself." The Revolution was the source of "the germ which has vegetated, and still is to grow and expand into the universal liberty of mankind."[10] Transformed and institutionalized in constitutions, revolutionary natural right provided the basis for healthy republican government, improvements in society, and a more perfect union. According to political scientist Michael Zuckert, the Revolution opened up for Lincoln the possibility of bringing moral-reform ends into modern political life, giving rise to a "new politics of 'perfect liberty.'"[11]

The Federal Principle

The evolution of Lincoln's political thought in the 1840s took into account a second basic feature of revolutionary constitutionalism, the federal principle. Americans were one people whose national existence assumed the constitutional form of thirteen republican states. Initially under the Articles of Confederation, then in a more developed form under the Constitution of 1787, the American Union was a republic of republics. In the words of *Federalist* No. 39, the political system created by the Constitution was "partly federal, partly national," with government sovereignty effectively divided between the states and the general government.

By necessity as much as by choice, under the federal principle the identity of the "popular sovereign" whose consent gave legitimacy to government remained ambiguous. In the view of states' rights theorists, *the people of the several states*, independently of one another, ratified the Constitution as a compact among sovereign political communities. In the nationalist view, stated by Chief Justice John Marshall in *McCulloch v. Maryland* (1819), *the people of the United States* ratified the Constitution, acting in state conventions. And "where else should they have assembled?" Marshall asked. "No political dreamer was ever wild enough to think of breaking down the lines which separate the States, and of compounding the American people into one common mass."

Lincoln was not a political dreamer. At no time did he think of breaking down "the lines which separate the states," even during the Civil War, when revolutionary conditions offered the possibility of doing so. Lincoln's commitment to the constitutional system of federal democracy as the principle of American nationality placed him in opposition to politicians who may justly be described as "political dreamers": states' rights advocates who conflated and elevated state and popular sovereignty into a doctrine of imperious command calculated to destroy the compound republic that the framers of the Constitution had established.

The problem of designing a system of equal representation for individuals, local communities, and states was far more complex under the federal principle than in a unitary government, and as the number of states increased from thirteen to thirty-four by 1861, the complications increased greatly. No clear and exclusive focus existed for political action to protect the rights and liberties of the people. Creative constructions of the federal principle were possible where both state and federal governments, under the Declaration of Independence, claimed authority to protect the rights and interests of citizens. In practice, the line of demarcation between state and federal powers was often indistinct.

Ambiguity in the nature of the Union gave moral and cultural significance to abstract questions of political theory. How and to what extent were individuals represented in the government of the Union and in state governments? How and to what extent were states represented in the government of the Union? In what form was the consent of the people to be obtained and, as public opinion, transmitted to government as a source of obligation? In the debate over these questions, rival conceptions of state and national popular sovereignty arose. Depending on the extent to which they were taken—which in turn was related to the moral salience of the policy issues involved—these competing doctrines of popular sovereignty had the potential to undermine legitimate authority in either the states or the general government, leading to dissolution of the Union.

Before the 1830s, conflicts over socio-economic developmental issues were not serious enough to threaten the underlying moral consensus required for the conduct of representative self-government based on majority rule. This began to change in 1845, when the annexation of Texas, followed by the expansion of U.S. territory resulting from the Mexican War, thrust slavery into national politics. Political and moral opinion polarized along sectional lines, raising the specter of disintegration of the Union.

Three Views of Popular Sovereignty

During the critical period 1846 to 1860, three conceptions of popular sovereignty were invoked in the controversy over the extension of slavery into the territories and in the broader debate over the place of slavery in the nation as a whole. The first was that of Senator Stephen A. Douglas of Illinois, who advocated a form of popular sovereignty that would allow the people of a territory to decide the slavery question for themselves. The second was that of pro-slavery southerners, who insisted that all questions concerning slavery—both immediate and long term—were subject to final decision by the people of the slave states, who were constitutionally and morally justified in acting in any way necessary for their self-preservation. Lincoln and the Republican party adopted a third position: the traditional idea of popular sovereignty as defined and structured in the Constitution, the partly federal–partly national system of the framers.

Advocates of each view claimed constitutional sanction. What set Lincoln's position apart was his belief that the idea of popular self-government was limited not only by the Constitution but also by a moral standard of reason and justice. Although ideally the nation's Constitution might be seen as aspiring to such a standard, in actuality its moral judgment of slavery was qualified by compromises that recognized the existence of slavery as a state institution, and that gave the southern states a political advantage by including their slaves in the system of representation. But outside the jurisdiction of the states, in territories where slavery did not exist, the situation was different. There, suspension of a moral judgment of slavery was not required. The principles of the Constitution could be applied with greater fidelity to the true meaning of popular self-government as understood in the light of the Declaration of Independence.

Lincoln's awareness of the moral tensions produced by the slavery controversy can be seen in his assessment of sectional politics after the annexation of Texas. He wrote in 1845: "I hold it to be a paramount duty of us in the free states, due to the Union of the states, and perhaps to liberty itself (paradox though it may seem) to let the slavery of the other states alone." On the other hand, he said, "I hold it to be equally clear, that we should never knowingly lend ourselves directly or indirectly, to prevent that slavery from dying a natural death—to find new places for it to live in, when it can no longer exist in the old." And beyond the controversy between free and slave states was the deeper question of the right of revolution, which Lincoln recognized in observing: "Of course I am not now considering what would be our duty, in cases of insurrection among the slaves."[12]

SLAVERY IN THE TERRITORIES

Lincoln applied his understanding of representative self-government with increasing clarity and force in the conflict over territorial slavery triggered by the acquisition of land from Mexico after the Mexican War (1846–48). Lincoln first resisted the popular-sovereignty doctrine of Douglas, enacted as congressional policy in the Compromise of 1850 (which admitted California as a free state but created the territories of New Mexico and Utah with no restriction on slavery) and the Kansas-Nebraska Act of 1854 (which left decisions about slavery in the territories to the residents). In 1861 Lincoln faced a still more serious popular-sovereignty challenge in the form of secession from the Union by seven states acting in popular conventions.

In opposing Douglas's doctrine of popular sovereignty between 1854 and 1860, Lincoln explored the meaning of representative democracy with philosophical depth and rhetorical power. His conflict with Douglas concerned the problem of identifying public opinion as the consent of the people that imposed obligation on government.

Douglas contended that the 1854 Kansas-Nebraska Act merely reaffirmed "the popular will" in favor of repeal of the slavery-restriction line drawn in the 1820 Missouri Compromise. That will was seen, Douglas said, in the 1850 legislation creating the New Mexico and Utah territories without restriction on slavery. But Lincoln, asserting that public opinion was *against* opening national territory to slavery, said the 1820 legislative restriction on slavery had become "canonized in the hearts of the people." It could not therefore, "in any reasonable mind, be understood that the Compromises of 1850 were meant and intended to disturb it."[13] Here Lincoln used public opinion to mean a firmly embedded conviction or sentiment in support of an established government policy.

Discussing political strategy, Lincoln said the existence of a Senate majority in support of the Kansas-Nebraska Act made its repeal impossible. Accordingly, critics of popular sovereignty aimed not to reenact the Missouri line but to bring about "the immediate and effectual restoration of it by popular sentiment." This was possible: "Let the decided demonstration of the Free States secure it." If the constituents of pro–Nebraska Act senators clearly expressed their will *against* the Nebraska Act, Lincoln urged, "will these senators disregard their will? Will they neither obey, nor make room for those who will?" "But even if we fail to technically restore the compromise," he said, "it is still a great point to carry a popular vote in favor of the restoration. The moral weight of such a restoration can not be estimated too highly."[14] Lincoln referred to public opinion in the form of elections, as well as, presumably, speeches, newspaper editorials, and pamphlets opposing Douglas's doctrine of popular sovereignty. The settled conviction of the nation in support of natural liberty outside the area of slave-state jurisdiction would then be fully recovered.

Self-Government and the Territories

The debate over public opinion pointed to the larger question of the nature of constitutional popular sovereignty. Under the federal principle, where did the power of self-government regarding slavery in the territories reside?

In Lincoln's view, Congress, representing the people of the whole country, had the authority to make law in new communities on public domain. "Is not Nebraska, while a territory, a part of us?" he asked. "Do we not own the country? And if we surrender the control of it, do we not surrender the right of self-government?" Lincoln believed the Nebraska territory was "part of ourselves"—the people of the United States—and hence subject to the legislative authority of Congress. He considered the counterargument that the government of the Union should not control the territory "because it is ONLY part." But if that were to be construed as a constitutional rule, it would vitiate legitimate national popular sovereignty. Observed Lincoln: "The same is true of every other part; and when all the parts are gone, what has become of the whole? What is then left of us? What use for the general government, when there is nothing left for it [to] govern?"[15]

Lincoln thus saw in the logic of territorial popular sovereignty a tendency toward the disintegration of the federal Union as the constitutional expression of representative government. In the immediate context, the question of self-government was of obvious concern to the country's black population, for whatever policy was adopted in the territories would have implications for slavery in the states. When Lincoln declared slavery a total violation of the principle of consent, and said, "Allow ALL the governed an equal voice in the government, and that, and that only is self government," he drew out those implications with unmistakable clarity.

Of greater political import, and equal moral cogency, was the fact that territorial popular sovereignty would deepen the corruption of the consent principle in the Constitution necessitated by the existence of slavery. The disposition of the territorial question affected constitutional relations between the slave and free states, relations that were degrading to the latter because of the three-fifths rule for representing the slave population in the House of Representatives. This gave a distinct advantage to slave states, making "each white man in South Carolina . . . more than the double of any man in Maine." There was not a voter in a slave state who did not have "more legal power in the government, than any voter in any free State," Lincoln noted.

Lincoln accepted the three-fifths rule because it was in the Constitution.

> But when I am told that I must leave it altogether to OTHER PEOPLE to say whether new partners are to be bred up and brought into the firm, on the same degrading terms against me, I respectfully demur. I insist, that whether I shall be a whole man, or only, the half of one, in comparison with others, is a question in which I am somewhat concerned; and one which no other man can have a sacred right of deciding for me. . . . If there is ANYTHING which it is the duty of the WHOLE PEOPLE to never entrust to any hands but their own, that thing is the preservation and perpetuity, of their own liberties, and institutions.

In effect Lincoln put proponents of popular sovereignty on notice that by opening national territory to slavery, they invited political agitation against a rule of representation that was adopted as a matter of political necessity in the formation of the Constitution, but in the opinion of many should now be treated as a matter of political and moral choice.[16]

The Limits of Public Opinion

Both sides in the struggle over slavery claimed to represent the will of the people. Lincoln was at once keenly aware of the wisdom and *necessity* of basing government on the consent of the people as expressed in public opinion, and keenly aware of the *difficulty* in a free society of knowing what public opinion is. More than that, he was aware of the limits of genuine public opinion—to say nothing of ungenuine opinion—as a source of obligation for government. Public opinion consisted in central ideas of an objective, rational, and universal nature whose persuasive power informed the views of individual citizens. But not all universal sentiments could be accepted as true, and central ideas that *were* true could be denied, distorted, or otherwise expunged from public opinion and replaced by wrong and irrational ideas. Lincoln believed that the latter situation described American politics in the 1850s. Democratic popular sovereignty posed the danger that politicians, out of partisan and ideological motives, would seek to manipulate citizens' views, corrupting and transforming genuine public opinion.

Lincoln believed that passage of the Kansas-Nebraska Act was an act of violence, not law, that corrupted public opinion. The act was carried by senators' votes "in violent disregard of the known will of their constituents," and it was maintained in violence when subsequent elections showing a clear demand for its repeal were disregarded. Lincoln related as a matter of personal knowledge an account of Douglas's giving orders in a Democratic party caucus in the Illinois legislature that changed almost unanimous opposition into overwhelming support for the Nebraska Act. "The masses too, democratic as well as whig, were even nearer unanimous against it," Lincoln said, but "as soon as the party necessity of supporting it became apparent, the way the democracy began to see the *wisdom* and *justice* of it, was perfectly astonishing." Public support of the Kansas-Nebraska Act was obtained "not in a sense of right, but in the teeth of a sense of wrong, to *sustain Douglas*," he charged.[17]

Lincoln feared the corrupting effect of popular sovereignty. In December 1856 he disputed the claim of President Franklin Pierce that the election of Democrat James Buchanan, with a plurality of the popular vote, expressed the will of the people. "Our government rests in public opinion," Lincoln observed, and "whoever can change public opinion, can change the government, practically just so much." Public opinion "always has a '*central idea*,' from which all its minor thoughts radiate," and in

American "political public opinion" the central idea had always been "'the equality of men.'" But Buchanan's election, Lincoln argued, signaled an intention to establish the opposite idea, that slavery is right and ought to be perpetuated and extended "to all countries and colors."[18]

In the debates with Douglas in 1858, Lincoln reflected further on public opinion. "In this and like communities, public sentiment is everything," he stated. "With public sentiment, nothing can fail; without it nothing can succeed. Consequently, he who moulds public sentiment, goes deeper than he who enacts statutes or pronounces decisions. He makes statutes and decisions possible or impossible to be executed." Until the Kansas-Nebraska Act, Lincoln said, "the whole public mind, that is the mind of the great majority," rested in the hope and belief that slavery was on its way to extinction. That was Lincoln's personal belief, too. "For that reason," he acknowledged, although he had always been opposed to slavery, "it had been a minor question with me." But now it was necessary to recover and reinforce in the public mind the belief that slavery would eventually disappear. Keeping slavery out of national territories would accomplish this purpose, ending the sectional crisis. Slavery could be left alone for a hundred years, Lincoln speculated, "if it should live so long, in the States where it exists."[19]

No Right to Do Wrong

Although willingness to project a century-long process of emancipation might suggest moral laxity rather than fervor, throughout the debate over territorial slavery Lincoln provoked controversy by emphasizing the relationship between moral standards and popular self-government. Beyond the problem of determining the content of public opinion, he said in attacking Douglas in 1854, was the question whether repeal of the Missouri Compromise, with its avowed principle of popular sovereignty, was "intrinsically right." The doctrine of self-government, referring to the right of individuals and communities to do as they pleased with all that was exclusively their own, "is right—absolutely and eternally right," said Lincoln. Yet "it has no just application" in the Kansas-Nebraska Act. "Or . . . whether it has such just application depends upon whether a negro is *not* or *is* a man," he reasoned. If the Negro is a man, then it is "a total destruction of self-government, to say that he shall not govern *himself*."[20]

Douglas professed moral indifference to the fate of slavery in the territories; any community that wanted slaves could have them. Lincoln said this was true if slavery was not a wrong. But if slavery *was* a wrong, then Douglas was in error, for "he cannot say people have a right to do wrong." Douglas held that slaves should be allowed in the territories just as other property was. This was logical if slave property and other property were equal. "But if you insist that one is wrong, and the other right," reasoned Lincoln, "there is no use to institute a comparison between right and wrong." "That is the real issue," he declared: "the eternal struggle between these two principles—right and wrong—throughout the world." When this fact was grasped, public opinion would recover its bearings and have its proper effect. Lincoln summarized:

> That will help the people to see where the struggle really is. It will hereafter place with us all men who do wish the wrong may have an end. And whenever we can get rid of the fog which obscures the real question—when we can get Judge Douglas and his friends to avow a policy looking to [slavery's] perpetuation—we can get out from among them that class of men and bring them to the side of those who treat it as a wrong. Then there will be an end of it, and that end will be its "ultimate extinction."[21]

Lincoln seems almost an Enlightenment rationalist in his confidence that reason and truth can inform and sustain public opinion as the moral ground of representative government. In this conception the task of the statesman is so to shape public deliberation that issues are "distinctly made," with "all extraneous matter thrown out so that men can fairly see the real difference between the parties."[22]   Alas, the controversy was to have a different resolution than what Lincoln envisioned in the contest with Douglas. What confuted his calculation was the willingness of pro-slavery politicians to put into practice an even more radical doctrine of popular sovereignty in the form of secession.

THE SECESSION CRISIS

In 1856, assessing his party's chances in the fight to defeat the admission of Kansas as a slave state, Lincoln said, "[W]e may be beaten. If we are, I shall not, on that account, attempt to dissolve the Union."[23] But southerners reached a different conclusion after the election of 1860 made Lincoln president. Claiming a constitutional right to withdraw from the Union, seven states repealed their ratification of the Constitution. The challenge facing Lincoln was to meet this extraordinary exercise in direct democracy while upholding his constitutional duty to carry out the will of the people as expressed in the 1860 election.

Secession presented itself as the act not of a state government but of the sovereign people of a state acting in their original constitutional capacity. According to this view, delegates elected to state conventions did not *represent* the people—they *were* the people. Secession was an exercise in direct democracy, the action of the people as a collective whole. The stark simplicity of the claim obscured its real meaning as a construction of the federal principle. In fact as well as in theory, states within the Union remained sovereign and independent, despite the appearance of limitations on state sovereignty. Secessionist logic meant that state citizens and officers were never bound in conscience to obey the laws of the Union; they had a moral and legal right to disobey those laws if they saw fit to do so. If state governments appeared to obey the laws of the Union, this was accidental or a matter of expediency, not an expression of moral obligation. In a moral and constitutional sense, states in the Union possessed perfect independence of action.[24]

Heeding the Voice of the People

Lincoln viewed the claim of a right of secession as a constitutional absurdity, the logical extension of the Democrats' halfway doctrine of *territorial* popular sovereignty. Against it he appealed to the constitutional orthodoxy of *national* popular sovereignty, institutionally defined and distributed throughout the Union under the forms of the federal principle. The election that made him president was an authoritative expression of the will of the people, and it imposed political and moral obligation on the government. It transmitted public opinion to government in a manner compatible with the exercise of executive authority under the Constitution according to the president's prudential judgment. Indeed, Lincoln believed that under the circumstances his surrender of his obligation to exercise authority would amount to a destruction of constitutional government.

Although in all but a formal, party-platform sense, disunion had been the main issue in the presidential election, secession created a constitutional crisis for which no one was fully prepared. To deal with it required political prudence more than legal virtuosity. Lincoln and the Republican party were under great pressure to indicate policy to be adopted toward the seceding states. Politicians devised methods of securing the sense of the people in the radically altered political situation, as though the outcome of the election shed no light on the subject. A special compromise committee in the Senate devised a proposal to establish territorial slavery under a series of constitutional amendments. Supporters recommended that states hold special elections "to enable the whole people" to vote on the compromise proposals.[25] Measures were introduced into Congress calling for a national constitutional convention to permit the people to express their will on the crisis of the Union. When it was clear that no such bill could pass, Virginia called a convention, attended by twenty-one border and northern states, to frame a compromise expressing the public desire to avoid war.

Throughout the secession winter, Lincoln resisted efforts to expand the idea of public opinion beyond the scope of its formal constitutional expression.[26] He adopted a rhetorical strategy of silence, intended to recognize the authoritative scope of constitutionally defined public opinion and his duties and responsibility as president-elect. His constitutional responsibility prevented him from revising positions on the basis of which he had been elected. Describing such a course as "dishonorable and treacherous," Lincoln said: "I will suffer death before I will consent . . . to any concession or compromise which looks like buying the privilege of taking possession of the government to which we have a constitutional right." To surrender to the demand that he appease his enemies would "break the only bond of faith between public, and public servant" and "distinctly set the minority over the majority." This was a question not merely of personal honor but of the preservation of constitutional government.[27]

Underscoring the obligation placed upon him by the people's judgment in the presidential election, Lincoln affirmed his trust in the will of the people as giving basic direction to the government. Southerners as well as northerners expressed devotion to the Constitution, provided their rights were upheld under it. "The question is, as to what the Constitution means—what are their rights under the Constitution?" Lincoln asked: "To decide that, who shall be the judge? Can you think of any other, than the voice of the people?"[28]

Lincoln's Inaugural Address

At length, after months of the most intense anticipation, Lincoln spoke about the national crisis in his inaugural address, March 4, 1861. He offered his considered judgment on the nature of the Union, representative self-government, and secession and revolution as instruments of popular sovereignty for altering or abolishing government. "I hold, that in contemplation of universal law, and the Constitution, the Union of these States is perpetual," he declared. The Union—the government of the nation—was, like all national governments, intended to enjoy permanent existence by obvious implication of its fundamental law, the Constitution of the United States.

The leading object of the Constitution was to strengthen the ties between the states, forming them into "a more perfect Union." Perfectness of Union as a principle of obligation in constitutional law, according to Lincoln, meant that one state, or "a part only, of the States," could not lawfully destroy the Union. Union-making was a one-way street, a constructive, not a destructive, project. Perfectness of Union implied the goodness of the existence of the nation as a living thing, the end of which was growth and development in human freedom and self-government. On this understanding of the country's reason for being, Lincoln declared that "no State, upon its own mere motion, can lawfully get out of the Union."[29]

Lincoln's position was not simply that sound principles of government do not allow the disintegration of government, or that the obligation to obey law in a political community cannot coexist with a right to disobey the same law. In defending the Union, Lincoln argued that republican government, rightly understood, precludes the claim of a constitutional right of secession. To establish this proposition he had to show the heretical nature of secession in relation both to the right of revolution and to the principles of compact, the two theoretical traditions in which disunion might be justified.

Although secession was mainly defended as a form of political action constitutionally protected from interference by the federal government or any other state, some southerners viewed it as an exercise of the right of revolution under the Declaration of Independence. In practical terms, moreover, secession was widely perceived as revolution. Lincoln was therefore obliged to consider the crisis from the standpoint of the right of revolution, the ultimate expression of popular sovereignty.

"If, by the mere force of numbers, a majority should deprive a minority of any clearly written constitutional right," Lincoln said, "it might in a moral point of view, justify revolution." This would certainly be true if the right in question was a "vital one." But that was not the case. "All the vital rights of minorities, and of individuals, are so plainly assured to them, by affirmations and negations, guarranties [sic] and prohibitions, in the Constitution, that controversies never arise concerning them." Lincoln recognized the right of revolution as an attribute of popular sovereignty. Although "physically speaking" division of the nation was impossible, he nevertheless acknowledged: "This country, with its institutions, belongs to the people who inhabit it. Whenever they shall grow weary of the existing government, they can exercise their *constitutional* right of amending it, or their *revolutionary* right to dismember, or overthrow it." [30]

To complete his defense of the Union, Lincoln considered the constitutionality of secession from the standpoint of the theory of compact. If "the United States be not a government proper, but an association of States in the nature of a contract merely, can it, as a contract, be peaceably unmade, by less than all the parties who made it?" he asked. "One party to a contract may violate it—break it, so to speak; but does it not require all to lawfully rescind it?"[31] The conciseness of this objection to secession does not detract from its significance. From the time of the nullification crisis, many compact theorists had argued that individual state secession was unconstitutional, and that joint action of the states was required to deratify the Constitution, as it had been to ratify it. If the difficulty of obtaining majority approval for a dissolution of the Union ensured the practical disutility of this procedure, this could be viewed as a necessary restraint on the exercise of the people's sovereignty.

In the revolutionary tradition that formed the ground of his project for preserving the rights and liberties of the people, Lincoln's signal achievement was to establish the right of resistance to unjustified revolution.[32] To claim secession as either a revolutionary or a constitutional right was a false and treacherous form of popular sovereignty. Lincoln summarized: "Plainly, the central idea of secession, is the essence of anarchy. A majority, held in restraint by constitutional checks, and limitations, and always changing easily, with deliberate changes of popular opinions and sentiments, is the only true sovereign of a free people." Considering unanimity impossible and the rule of the minority "inadmissible" as a permanent arrangement, Lincoln said that whoever rejected the rule of the constitutional majority "does, of necessity, fly to anarchy or to despotism."[33]

Lincoln underscored the authority of the people to determine the outcome of the crisis. Noting that under the Constitution the people conferred no authority on the president to fix the terms for the separation of the states, he said they could do this if they chose. Meanwhile, "[w]hy should there not be a patient confidence in the ultimate justice of the people?" he asked. "Is there any better, or equal hope, in the world?" Yet the sovereignty of the people was subject to a higher authority. "If the Almighty Ruler of nations, with his eternal truth and justice, be on your side of the North, or on yours of the South," Lincoln said, "that truth, and that justice, will surely prevail, by the judgment of this great tribunal, the American people." Stressing the boundaries of the executive power, Lincoln recognized the decisive yet limited ways in which, in the design of the Constitution, consent of the people was intended to impose obligation on government.[34]

The War: Secession as Rebellion

The secessionists resolved the crisis of the Union by firing the first shot at Fort Sumter. This action was the "appeal to heaven" recognized in the theory of revolutionary resistance. By successfully treating secession as rebellion, Lincoln was able to show that the Union was a true government.[35] He answered the Confederate attack with the proclamation of April 15, 1861, calling the militia, convening Congress, and appealing to all loyal citizens to aid the effort to maintain "the existence of our National Union, the perpetuity of popular government; and to redress wrongs already long enough endured."[36]

The conduct of the war confirmed and clarified the principles of popular self-government for which the war was fought. In relation to public opinion and the people's consent, the most significant issue was the difficulty of deciding the identity of the people and of judging whether it was necessary, for military purposes, to circumscribe the operation of the majority principle.

Lincoln acknowledged this issue in July 1861, when he promised government aid to loyal citizens of Virginia claiming protection against the rebellion. "Those loyal citizens, this government is bound to recognize and protect, as being Virginia," he declared.[37] Two years later Lincoln affirmed the principle in approving as constitutional the formation of the state of West Virginia out of Virginia. It is not merely qualified voters but rather qualified voters who choose to vote "that constitute the political power of the state," he said. "Can this government stand," he asked, "if it indulges constitutional constructions by which men in open rebellion against it, are to be accounted, man for man, the equals of those who maintain their loyalty to it?" It was said that the admission of West Virginia was secession, "and tolerated only because it is our secession." Observed Lincoln: "Well, if we call it by that name, there is still difference enough between secession against the constitution and secession in favor of the constitution."[38]

During the war Lincoln adopted a policy of reconstruction that encouraged loyal citizens to resume political activity for the sake of the Union, even though they were a minority of the pre-war population. Because secession was a constitutional nullity, the loyal minority must represent a rebellious state in its present disorganized condition. The consent of the minority was needed, not to give direction to government policy in militarily occupied regions, but as a sign that public opinion— in a principled and ideal sense—was on the side of constitutional liberty and republican government.

Lincoln was assassinated just at the time when the issue of majority rule and minority rights under the consent principle was to be posed in even more novel, ambiguous, and intractable political circumstances. Given his success in meeting the challenge of Democratic popular sovereignty and secessionist direct democracy, we may reasonably conclude that, both prudentially and in principle, Lincoln grasped the true meaning of representative government and the role of public opinion in a well-ordered constitutional regime. That his statesmanship would have had an ameliorating effect on Reconstruction politics, as his teaching and example may yet have on our own political distemper, is not idle speculation.

CHAPTER FOUR

Beyond Referendum Democracy: Competing Conceptions of Public Opinion

James S. Fishkin

For more than two hundred years, American democratic theory—and practice—has wrestled with a fundamental dilemma. Superficially, that dilemma might seem to pose a choice between representative democracy and increasingly direct forms of public consultation. While there is some merit in construing the choice that way, I propose to frame it differently: in terms of the contrasting forms of public opinion expressed by two kinds of democratic institutions.

The hard choice for the design (and possible reform) of democratic processes is, ultimately, between institutions that express what the public *actually* thinks but under debilitated conditions for thinking about the issue in question, and institutions that express what the public *would* think about the issue given better conditions for thinking about it. The choice, in other words, is between *debilitated but actual* opinion and *deliberative but counterfactual* opinion. One sort of institution offers a snapshot of public opinion as it is; another expresses what public opinion would be if the public were more informed, engaged, and attentive.

James S. Fishkin holds the Patterson-Banister Chair in Government, Law, and Philosophy at the University of Texas. He has doctorates in both political science and philosophy, from Yale (1975) and Cambridge (1976). His books include *The Voice of the People* (1995), *The Dialogue of Justice* (1993), *Democracy and Deliberation* (1991), and *Justice, Equal Opportunity, and the Family* (1983), all published by Yale University Press.

The first option is exemplified by the institutions of plebiscitary democracy—initiatives, referendums, public opinion polls, focus groups.[1] Moves to more direct consultation—say, through direct election of senators rather than the original indirect method—are also moves toward more plebiscitary democracy. Another such move is the transformation of the electoral college into a vote-aggregation mechanism, in contrast to the originally envisioned function of serving, state by state, as a deliberative body. Similarly, the dramatic increase in the use of the direct primary for selection of presidential candidates, particularly after the McGovern-Fraser reforms in the 1970s, has been a move toward more plebiscitary democracy. National party conventions were once institutions of elite deliberation, engaged in serious discussion of issues and party platforms and in multiple balloting for candidate selection. Now they are media extravaganzas, staged for their effects on mass public opinion; by the time they are held, the presidential candidates have already been determined by plebiscitary democracy—through direct primaries.

The second option is built into our concepts of deliberative and representative institutions. At their best, such institutions are sensitive not just to what constituents actually think but to what they would think if they were better informed. Later, I will discuss a new institutional strategy that more explicitly functions in this second way.

This distinction between the two forms of public opinion corresponds only roughly to the distinction between direct and representative democracy. One of the most influential institutions of plebiscitary democracy is the public opinion poll. While polls are closely aligned with direct democracy (and were originally offered by George Gallup as a proxy for direct democracy—even to the point of being called "sampling referendums"[2]), they use statistical samples to stand for, or represent, the public as a whole. The members of such a sample are selected by a random scientific process rather than by an election. But they are still "representative" of the mass public; they are a small body that stands for the rest.

A great deal of social-science evidence has been accumulated to support the view that individual citizens, most of the time, are "rationally ignorant" about politics and public affairs.[3] Each citizen in the large nation state knows that his or her vote, being only one of millions, will not make much difference, and so there is little incentive to pay close attention or to become informed. All of us have other things to do in which we can make more of a difference than we can with our one vote in millions. This lack of incentive for individual citizens to become seriously informed, engaged, or even attentive is regrettable from the standpoint of democratic theory. We would like citizens to be knowledgeable about the different positions of candidates in an election, or the arguments for and against a referendum proposal. However, a host of empirical evidence shows that this is rarely the case.

Corresponding to these differing notions of public opinion are differing views of the function of democratic institutions. The Founders used the metaphor of the *filter*: representative institutions were supposed to refine public opinion through the filter of deliberation. Opponents of elite filtering, beginning with the Anti-Federalists, relied on a different notion: representatives were to serve as a *mirror* of the public and its opinions. The filter creates deliberative but counterfactual representations of public opinion, while the mirror reflects public opinion just as it is.

The Filter

As Madison reported on his own position in his notes on the Constitutional Convention, he was "an advocate for the policy of refining the popular appointments by successive filtrations."[4] In *Federalist* 10 he argued that the effect of representation was "to refine and enlarge the public views by passing them through the medium of a chosen body of citizens. . . . Under such a regulation it may well happen that the public voice, pronounced by the representatives of the people, will be more consonant to the public good than if pronounced by the people themselves, if convened for the purpose." Running throughout Madison's thinking is the distinction between "refined" public opinion—that is, the considered judgments that can result from the deliberations of a small representative body—and the "temporary errors and delusions" of public opinion to be found outside this deliberative process. Only through the deliberations of a small, face-to-face, representative body can we arrive at the "the cool and deliberate sense of the community" (*Federalist* 63). This was a principal motivation for setting up the Senate, which was intended to resist the passions and interests that might divert the public into majority tyranny.

The Founders were sensitive to the social conditions that would make deliberation possible. For example, large meetings of citizens were considered dangerous because, no matter how thoughtful or virtuous the citizenry might be, large meetings could not be truly deliberative. As Madison said in *Federalist* 55, "had every Athenian citizen been a Socrates, every Athenian assembly would still have been a mob." The Founders' project of constitutional design was intended to create conditions in which the formulation and expression of deliberative public opinion would be possible.

The filter can be thought of as the process of deliberation whereby representatives arrive at considered judgments about public issues. For our purposes, then, a working notion of deliberation would be: face-to-face discussion in which participants raise and respond to competing arguments so as to form considered judgments about the solutions to public problems. If the group is too large, or if the participants are distracted by the kinds of passions or interests that would motivate factions, then deliberative democracy will not be possible. From the Founders' perspective, then, the social conditions we are familiar with in plebiscitary or referendum democracy would be far from appropriate for deliberation.

The Mirror

As Jack Rakove has noted, the one widely shared desideratum in the American notion of representation at the time of the founding was that a representative assembly should, to use John Adams's phrase, be "in miniature an exact portrait of the people at large."[5] In the hands of the Anti-Federalists, this notion became a basis for objecting to the apparent elitism of the filtering metaphor: only the educated upper classes, meeting in small elite assemblies, were expected to do the refining.

The mirror notion of representation was an expression of fairness and equality. As the "Federal Farmer" put it: "A fair and equal representation is that in which the interests, feelings, opinions, and views of the people are collected, in such manner as they would be were the people all assembled."[6] Melancton Smith, who opposed the Constitution at the New York ratification convention (and who may well have been the "Federal Farmer"), argued that representatives "should be a true picture of the people, possess a knowledge of their circumstances and their wants, sympathize in all their distresses, and be disposed to seek their true interests." In line with the mirror theory of representation, Anti-Federalists sought frequent elections, term limits, and any other measures that would increase the resemblance between representatives and those they represented.

"The people all assembled," to use the Federal Farmer's phrase, is exactly the kind of gathering the Federalists believed would give only an inferior rendering of the public good. Recall Madison's claim that a small representative group would give a better account of the public good than would the "people themselves if convened for the purpose" (*Federalist* 10). The Framers were clearly disturbed by the possibility that factions aroused by passions or interests adverse to the rights of others could do very bad things. The image they feared seems to be some combination of the Athenian mob and Shays's rebellion. Part of the case for deliberative public opinion is that the "cool and deliberate sense of the community" (*Federalist* 63) would be insulated from the passions and interests that might motivate factions. The Founders believed that public opinion when filtered by deliberative processes would be more likely to serve the public good and avoid mob-like behavior of the kind that threatens tyranny of the majority.

From the standpoint of the Framers, the conflict between the two forms of public opinion—and the institutions that would express them—was soon dramatized by the Rhode Island referendum, the only effort to consult the people directly about ratification of the Constitution. Rhode Island was a hotbed of paper money and, from the Federalist standpoint, irresponsible government and fiscal mismanagement. An Anti-Federalist stronghold, it lived up to the Founders' image of a place where the passions of the public, unfiltered by deliberation, might lead to dangerous results.

The Anti-Federalists sparked a thoroughgoing debate over the proper method of consulting the people. Referendum advocates held that submitting a question "to every Individual Freeholder of the state was the only Mode in which the true Sentiments of the people could be collected."[7] But the Federalists objected that a referendum would not provide a forum in which the arguments could really be joined; it would produce defective deliberation. To hold the referendum in town meetings scattered throughout the state would mean that differing arguments would be offered in the various locations, and there would not be any shared sense of how the arguments offered in one place might be answered in another. "The sea-port towns cannot hear and examine the arguments of their brethren in the country on this subject, nor can they in return be possessed of our views thereof. . . . Each separate interest will act under an impression of private and local motives only, uninformed of those reasons and arguments which might lead to measures of common utility and public good."[8] Federalists held that only in a convention could representatives of the entire state meet together, voice their concerns, and have those concerns answered by persons with different views, so as to arrive at some collective solution for the common good. The very idea of the convention as a forum for ratification was an important innovation motivated by the need for deliberation.

Federalists also noted another defect in mass public opinion: lack of information. "Every individual Freeman ought to investigate these great questions to some good degree in order to decide on this Constitution: the time therefore to be spent in this business would prove a great tax on the freemen to be assembled in Town-meetings, which must be kept open not only three days but three months or more, in preparation as the people at large have more or less information." While representatives chosen for a convention might acquire the appropriate information reasonably quickly, to prepare "the people at large" would take an extraordinary amount of time.

In the end the Rhode Island referendum was held, it was boycotted by the Federalists, and the Constitution was voted down. But the state, under threat of embargo and even dismemberment (Connecticut was threatening to invade from one side and Massachusetts from the other), capitulated and held the required convention to approve the Constitution. This incident was an early salvo in a long American war of competing conceptions of democracy. Democratic institutions typically offer a mix of deliberative and plebiscitary democracy, a mix of the filter and the mirror, but over the last two centuries in America (and in most other developed democracies) the mix has shifted toward far greater plebiscitary influence.

The Role of Representatives

Madison's picture of deliberating representatives seems far removed from most of our political experience since the Founding. It is certainly far removed from the contemporary world of political parties, campaign contributions, television advertising, and candidates who function as issue entrepreneurs in an environment of near-perpetual campaigning. Madison lived at least part of his life in an era when letters from Virginia to Massachusetts would slowly make their way via England; he had no inkling that technology might transform politics by transforming political communication. Madison thought elections would be less subject to "the vicious arts" in large electorates than in small ones. He was thinking primarily of bribery, and it is of course harder to bribe a large population than a small one.[9] But the opportunities for demagoguery and manipulation of the public are clearly available in large electorates, particularly when technology makes communication to vast numbers so easy. The vicious arts, conceived more broadly than just bribery, may actually be easier to practice in large electorates, through the use of the media, than in very small ones where vestiges of face-to-face democracy remain.

Madison's notion that representatives "refine and enlarge the public's views by passing them through a chosen body of citizens" suggests a middle ground in the dilemma often facing representatives today.[10] That dilemma is usually framed as a choice between deferring to the wishes of constituents and making a substantive judgment. Should representatives follow the polls? Or should they vote their own views of what is best for the country (or their state or district)? Each option presents difficulties. If members of Congress follow the polls, they can be seen as mere weathervanes for the shifting winds of public opinion. But if they follow their own views when their constituents disagree, then they can be criticized for imposing their personal value judgments on an electorate that thinks otherwise.

A slight variation in the pattern of representatives' conforming to actual public opinion is to think of them not as weathervanes but as weather predictors: they attempt to predict what their constituents will think about an issue as it evolves. But from a normative standpoint this is not an improvement. On many issues the public will never be well informed and may even become increasingly misled. What the public would think if it could get some reasonable account of the relevant information is very different from what it is likely to think in an environment of attack ads and sound bites.

The middle position, between following the public's uninformed views and following the representative's more informed but (perhaps) merely personal views, is easily overlooked. The third way is that representatives can take account of what they think their constituents *would* think about an issue, once they got the facts and heard the arguments on both sides and had a reasonable chance to ponder the matter. This view provides grounds for resisting the pressure of polls on issues that the public knows little about. On the other hand, it is not the same as saying that the representative should simply vote his or her own views. The representative may know that his values differ from those of constituents on a given question, or that constituents would never accept a particular policy, even with a great deal more information and discussion. The representative may also know his constituents well enough to have some idea of what they would accept if only they had the information.

While this view of the representative's role is not often articulated, it does surface in rare moments when Congress is being self-conscious. Consider Samuel Beer's recommendations to the House Judiciary Committee during the preparations for the impeachment trial of President Clinton. Beer's claim was that the Congress is "a creature of the people . . . acting in lieu of the people between quadrennial elections. *At their best, the legislators will do what the people, at their best, would do.*"[11] Several members of Congress publicly rationalized their role in the impeachment process by referring to the same notion of what the people would think if they were as informed as the members.[12]

Impeachment is, of course, a rare and momentous event. The extent to which members might accept such a view of their role on more routine issues is an open question. For our purposes we need only note that this middle-ground position on the role of representatives expresses a normative claim of deliberative democracy, the aspiration to represent the public's considered judgments.

Does Deliberation Make a Difference?

If representatives "refined and enlarged" the public's views so as to represent what their constituents would want if they were better informed, would this really be much different from simply following conventional polls? Is refined public opinion really very different from mirrored public opinion? Some competing lines of recent research in political science shed light on this question.

One approach claims that deliberative or more informed public opinion would not make any difference. In this view, ordinary citizens use "cues" or "heuristics" as "shortcuts" to approximate the views they would hold if they became informed. Even if they are rationally ignorant, they use "low information rationality" to come to conclusions very similar to those they would arrive at if they spent the time and effort required to achieve "high information rationality." Samuel Popkin, Arthur Lupia, and others have made this argument.[13] Lupia, for example, applies it to a referendum on auto insurance in California, noting that once voters know who is for it and who is against it, they can figure out their own position. My colleague Robert Luskin calls this approach the "extenuationist theory" of public opinion. It admits that the public lacks information, at least if evaluated by elite standards, but seeks to minimize the implications of that ignorance.[14] The extenuationist theory is buttressed primarily by models and evidence derived from cross-sectional data, gathered from surveys of public opinion. Basically, people who are not well informed are compared to others with similar socio-demographic characteristics who are more informed, and it is assumed that the less informed would vote the way their more informed counterparts do.

A much more persuasive basis for claiming that information, engagement, or discussion either does or does not make much difference would be to subject a group of people who are not well informed or much engaged to an experiment in which they become more so, and then to see if that makes a difference in their views or voting intentions. For some years now, various colleagues and I have been involved in a research initiative called Deliberative Polling. This initiative has a variety of aims, one being to explore the impact of information and deliberation on voting intention.

Deliberative Polling begins with the mirror—using random, representative sampling to provide a statistical microcosm of the public. It then subjects the participants to the filter—an opportunity to deliberate under favorable conditions. After taking an initial survey, participants are invited for a weekend of face-to-face deliberation and are given carefully balanced briefing materials. They are randomly assigned to small groups for discussions with trained moderators who attempt to establish an atmosphere in which participants listen to one another and no one is allowed to dominate. They are then encouraged to take questions arising from the small-group discussions to larger plenary sessions where they can put them to competing experts and politicians. At the end of the weekend, the participants again take the survey they took at the beginning.[15]

In every case thus far, the weekend microcosm has been highly representative, both attitudinally and demographically, as compared to the entire baseline survey and to census data about the population. And in every case thus far, there have been large and statistically significant changes of opinion over the weekend. Considered judgments are often different from the top-of-the-head attitudes solicited by conventional polls.

But what do the results represent? Our respondents are able to overcome the usual incentives for rational ignorance. Instead of one vote in millions, they have, in effect, one vote in a few hundred in the weekend sample, and one voice in fifteen or so in the small-group discussions. They overcome apathy, disconnection, inattention, and lack of information. Participants from all social locations change through the deliberation; we cannot predict change by knowing that someone is educated or not, economically advantaged or not. We do know, however, that becoming informed on the issues is a predictor of change in policy attitudes. In that sense, deliberative public opinion is both informed and representative. As a result, it is almost inevitably counterfactual. The public is unlikely ever to become as informed and engaged as participants in our weekend microcosms.

The Deliberative Poll has been tried nearly twenty times in various parts of the world. There was a national version on PBS with the 1996 U.S. presidential candidates at the "National Issues Convention," anchored by Jim Lehrer. It was used in Britain at the time of the 1997 General Election and four other times, on TV Channel Four. And it has also been tried twice before national referendums: in Australia in 1999, before the referendum on Australia's becoming a republic, and in Denmark in 2000, before the referendum on adoption of the Euro.

The Australian Referendum

Perhaps the clearest context for considering the impact of deliberation is offered by the Australian Deliberative Poll, organized by Issues Deliberation Australia with help from the Center for Deliberative Polling at the University of Texas and many other entities.[16] The referendum posed a choice between (a) keeping the existing head of state, the Queen, as represented in Australia by the Governor General, and (b) changing to a President, to be nominated by the Prime Minister with the agreement of the Leader of the Opposition and approved by a two-thirds vote of Parliament. One of the interesting complexities is that the public, while overwhelmingly in favor of becoming a republic, also strongly favored direct election of the head of state by the people. This option was not on the ballot.

The choice offered in the referendum was set up about twenty months earlier, in a "Constitutional Convention" attended partly by political elites and partly by citizens elected for the purpose. Despite considerable divisions, a clear consensus did emerge: if there was to be a republic, it should be one in which the indirectly elected President would take over, more or less, the powers and responsibilities of the current Governor General.

The Madisonian theory of democracy holds that the appropriate context for deliberation is a small representative body, such as a convention, a senate, or the U.S. Electoral College as originally conceived. Only such small, deliberative bodies could filter the public views and make a considered judgment about the public interest. Indeed, the famous passage in _Federalist_ 10 that said representatives serve to "refine and enlarge the public's views" also asserted that the resulting "public voice" will be "more consonant to the public good than if pronounced by the people themselves, if convened for the purpose." Here is a stark statement about the contrast between the filter and the mirror. If we just ask the people, without a context of deliberation, we will get an inferior statement of the public good. But if we filter their views through a small deliberative body of representatives, then judgments "more consonant to the public good" will result.

The Australian referendum case is particularly notable because it offered a contrast of three decision-making processes: a constitutional convention, a national referendum, and a Deliberative Poll. The "extenuationist theory" would tell us that the results of a Deliberative Poll should not be much different from the results of a referendum. Voters do not need to take the time to deliberate and become informed; they can use "low information rationality," "cues," and "shortcuts" to come to the same conclusions. By contrast, the Madisonian theory would tell us that a properly functioning constitutional convention might offer the same kinds of conclusions as the public would arrive at if it could experience the same kind of deliberation, consider the issues, and become well informed. Such conclusions would indeed be different from those we obtained from the mass public _without_ deliberation. In this view, the Deliberative Poll and the constitutional convention should give comparable results, and those results should differ from the results of the referendum.

Strikingly, the latter is what took place. Polls of the mass public found a strong preference for the direct-election option. The participants in the Deliberative Poll began with the same preference and initially expressed little support for the indirect-election model that was to be voted on in the referendum. However, like the participants in the constitutional convention, they also did not want a partisan politician to be head of state. They wanted someone above the fray, in the mold of the

Governor General. As they deliberated over the weekend, they thought through how a direct-election system would work—who would be likely to win elections. They realized that the President in such a system would probably be a politician tied to one of the major parties, since only such a politician would be in a position to mount a successful direct-election campaign. Over the course of the weekend, these issues led them to change their ordering of preferences: support for direct election plummeted, and support for the proposed indirect model went way up.

The participants in the weekend were also dramatically more informed about the issues. They could answer basic questions about the Australian constitution and about the proposal for changing it. The mass public was, by contrast, ill informed in its answers to the same questions at the start of the process. By the end of the campaign, as judged by a separate survey, the public was somewhat better informed but not nearly so well informed as the sample in the Deliberative Poll.

At least in this case, deliberation in a small representative body, whether the constitutional convention or the Deliberative Poll, led to very different results from those in the referendum. The Deliberative Poll in the 1997 British General Election had produced similarly striking changes of opinion, showing that an informed and representative microcosm would come to different views than the public in a mass plebiscite.

But the Deliberative Poll held before the 2000 Danish referendum on the Euro provides a contrasting and cautionary note. While there were large changes of opinion on some of the issues, such as the likely effect of the Euro on the future of the Danish welfare state, there were not large shifts in voting intention. The context, however, suggests an interesting explanation. Denmark has held six national referendums on European issues in the last three decades. In the initial survey before the deliberative weekend, an overwhelming majority could answer nearly all the questions correctly. The Danes routinely demonstrate the most knowledge of European issues in comparable surveys of European public opinion, such as the Eurobarometer. And so the Deliberative Poll was not a test of whether Danish voters could approximate their informed opinions by means of "low information rationality," since they started out with high levels of information. After three decades of information campaigns and public discussion, the citizenry was relatively well informed on this particular set of issues.

This exception helps to prove the rule. To consider just how unusual such circumstances are is to realize that the incentives for rational ignorance will routinely lead to uninformed opinions in most circumstances where the institutions of plebiscitary democracy—polls, primaries, referendums—are applied. Under most circumstances we face the hard choice between the mirror and the filter—between debilitated but actual opinion, and deliberative but counterfactual opinion. The Deliberative Poll is an effort to give expression, influence, and visibility to the latter. But it is only the start of what should be an agenda of research and institutional experimentation aimed at keeping our reliance on non-deliberative, plebiscitary democracy within limits.

CHAPTER FIVE

Polling and the Creation of a Virtual Public

Benjamin Ginsberg

During the nineteenth and early twentieth centuries, American political struggles were mainly waged in the electoral arena. Full white male suffrage was achieved during the Jacksonian era, and those eligible to vote were highly mobilized. By the 1890s, voter turnout averaged nearly 80 per cent in presidential elections and approached 70 per cent in midterm congressional races. Outside the South turnout was even higher, exceeding 90 per cent in some areas.[1]

These high levels of voting participation reflected the fact that contending political forces conducted their battles largely through competitive electoral mobilization. Debates about policies and struggles for power among rival elites were not confined to the legislative chambers and cloakrooms of the Capitol. Instead, conflicts over such matters as the tariff, internal improvements, slavery, banks, monetary policy, and immigration generally spilled over into the electoral arena as opposing forces sought to secure victory in Washington by outmobilizing and outpolling their foes throughout the countryside.

Today, contending elites have found ways to achieve their aims and, when necessary, wage political warfare without resorting to popular

Benjamin Ginsberg is David Bernstein Professor of Political Science, director of the Center for the Study of American Government, and special assistant to the dean in the School of Arts and Sciences at Johns Hopkins University. Recent books include *Politics by Other Means: Politicians, Prosecutors and the Press from Watergate to Whitewater* (1999) and *American Government: Freedom and Power* (1999).

mobilization. Rather than seek to outpoll their opponents, contemporary elites practice "personal democracy," a form of political activity that does not require the active involvement of ordinary Americans.[2] Contending elites use litigation, administrative processes, and the choices given to them by school, pension, and housing programs to achieve their goals. The tens of millions of individuals who once constituted the lifeblood of American politics have become politically superfluous. They are increasingly integrated into the political process through "customer relations" rather than political mobilization. Note the famous 1993 "National Performance Review," which advises government agencies to treat citizens as "customers" but, significantly, never reminds them that their customers might actually own the store.[3]

The views of even politically superfluous Americans are, of course, heavily polled. Day after day, political parties and government agencies—to say nothing of the media and private corporations—conduct surveys on every conceivable political topic. But these should be seen as management tools designed to warn of potential trouble, rather than reflections of the importance of public opinion in the political process. Extensive surveys are part of the transformation of Americans from citizens to customers and the diminution of their role in political life.

POPULAR MOBILIZATION AND ITS ALTERNATIVES

Political historians have dubbed nineteenth-century American political campaigns as "militarist" in style.[4] Competing political parties were well organized and active in virtually every constituency in the nation. Voters in each precinct were "drilled" by party "captains," who received support and information from a disciplined and well-financed party organization. A rabidly partisan press disseminated news that sometimes amounted to little more than party propaganda.[5] Throughout the country, hundreds of thousands of party workers marched from house to house on election day, handing out leaflets, helping voters go to the polls, and even, upon occasion, offering financial incentives to voters who needed a bit of extra assistance in making up their minds.[6] Millions of citizens attended campaign rallies, listened to speeches, marched in parades, and actively took part in American political life.[7]

Political competition in nineteenth-century America was not solely a matter of electoral mobilization. America's first impeachment crisis, after all, occurred during the 1860s, and criminal indictments and prosecutions, such as those of the Whiskey Ring and Tweed Ring, were important weapons in political struggle throughout the century. Moreover, particularly in the South, violence by groups like the Ku Klux Klan played a major role in resolving political conflicts.[8] Nevertheless, all-out voter mobilization in national elections was a central strategy for forces seeking to control the government and influence policy.

The nineteenth-century pattern of lively public involvement is a far cry from the manner in which politics is conducted in contemporary America. For the past several decades, voter turnout in the United States has been extremely low, averaging slightly more than 50 per cent in presidential contests. Fewer than 49 per cent of those eligible actually voted in the 1996 presidential election, the lowest electoral turnout since 1924. In midterm congressional elections, more than two-thirds of eligible voters stay home. Generally speaking, affluent and well-educated Americans continue to vote. Except among younger persons, presidential-election turnout among college graduates averages close to 80 per cent. Less affluent and less well educated Americans, on the other hand, have been increasingly marginalized in the political process. Among those with less than a high school education, for instance, voter turnout has dropped from close to 50 per cent in the early 1970s to barely 30 per cent in the 1996 presidential race.[9]

Competing political forces in contemporary America obviously have not given up seeking to appeal to voters. Indeed, politicians spend enormous sums on election campaigns. Parties and candidates may have spent as much as $2 billion competing for popular support in the 1996 national, state, and local races and doubtless spent even more in 2000.[10] Much of this money typically buys television advertising during the final month of the campaign, advertising aimed at middle-class Americans who are already registered and likely to vote. Sophisticated polling techniques allow candidates to target very specific slices of this truncated and already mobilized audience with political advertising designed to appeal to their particular interests.[11] With the growth of computerized databases and greater candidate familiarity with the potential inherent in Internet advertising, targeted or "customized" campaigning is certain to become even more important in the years to come.[12]

The Failure to Mobilize

In 2000, both parties announced plans for get-out-the-vote campaigns, but both appeared to be limiting their efforts to established voters.[13] In sharp contrast with the nineteenth-century pattern, neither party makes much of an effort to defeat its opponents by attempting to mobilize the tens of millions of poorer and less-well-educated Americans who are not currently part of the electorate.[14] Indeed, many candidates work to further depress turnout through the use of "negative advertising" that disparages the opposition; this advertising is designed to discourage both nonvoters and supporters of the candidate's opponents from coming to the polls.[15] The prevalence of negative campaigning and smear tactics is one reason why many Americans claim to be too disgusted to participate in politics.[16] Only the occasional political outsider like Minnesota governor Jesse Ventura makes any real effort to bring nonvoters into the electorate.[17] Neither of the established parties even supports electoral reforms such as the elimination of voter-registration requirements and a shift from weekday to weekend voting—the norms throughout Western Europe. The European experience suggests that these two changes alone would appreciably boost electoral turnout.

The parties' failure to engage in all-out efforts to mobilize the more than 60 million Americans who could but do not vote in presidential elections is especially striking given the bitter political struggles of the past few decades, and given also the fact that since the 1960s neither major party has been able to win a decisive edge in the electoral arena. Despite the huge sums candidates and parties have spent campaigning for the support of existing voters, the results have been inconclusive, and control of the government has been divided for most of the past thirty years. Party divisions in Congress, as evinced by patterns of roll-call voting, have achieved levels not seen since the nineteenth century, while partisan struggles between Congress and the White House have reached an unprecedented degree of intensity. Democratic Congresses drove the Republican Richard Nixon from office and sought to do the same to Ronald Reagan. A Republican Congress impeached but failed to convict Democratic president Bill Clinton. Significantly, though, these ferocious elite struggles have not led either party to try to mobilize more voters. Instead, participation has continued to decline.

Abandoning the Neoclassical Model

This pattern of popular quiescence alongside intense elite struggle contradicts what might be called the neoclassical theory of political participation, which asserts that in a democratic polity, high levels of elite conflict will inevitably lead to increased rates of mass participation as contending forces vie for political support. Writing during the 1950s, E. E. Schattschneider referred to this phenomenon as "expanding the scope of the conflict" and said it was a central feature of democratic political processes. He argued that popular mobilization was most likely to be initiated by the losers in elite struggles, who hoped to change the outcome by enlarging the universe of participants.[18]

During much of the nineteenth century and portions of the twentieth, American political practices seemed to be generally consistent with the neoclassical model. The Jeffersonians, Jacksonians, and Republicans all expanded suffrage and brought new groups into the political process in an effort to overwhelm their opponents at the polls. During the 1930s, the New Dealers sought to solidify their political power by increasing the participation of working-class and ethnic voters. As recently as the 1960s, liberal Democrats strove to defeat the Republicans and overpower conservative forces within their own party by enacting the Voting Rights Act, which enfranchised millions of African Americans in the South, and by securing the passage of the Twenty-sixth Amendment, which gave the vote to 18-year-olds.

Contemporary political patterns, however, seem less consistent with the neoclassical model. An astonishing two-thirds of those eligible to vote did not take part in the November 1998 national elections, even though the Democratic and Republican parties were locked in a momentous battle over impeachment of the President. Indeed, despite their bitter fights, contending elites deliberately refrained from mobilizing legions of new supporters. "I don't think we ought to play to that crowd," said Rep. John Lindner of Georgia, chairman of the House Republican campaign committee, when asked if the GOP should seek to bring new voters to the polls in 1998.[19] A decade earlier, Walter Mondale's advisors told him that the idea of mobilizing new voters was "backward thinking,"[20] and Democrats did not engage in large-scale voter-registration efforts even though the polls indicated that, among Americans registered and likely to vote, Mondale faced nearly certain defeat at the hands of Ronald Reagan.

Fear of Mobilization

Politicians have always been afraid to mobilize new voters. Expanding the universe of participants is seen as a risky strategy. Even in an era of scientific opinion polling, the political leanings of new participants are always uncertain. Democrats in the 1960s pushed for the 18-year-old vote only to discover that young voters helped the Republicans in the 1970s and 1980s.

Moreover, even if they remain loyal to the political party that mobilized them, new participants are likely to bring with them new aspirants for party leadership positions. Political leaders who succeed in bringing in new voters may find themselves watching the final victory of their cause from the sidelines. The popular forces brought into politics by the Jeffersonians, for example, dismayed their distinguished patrons by demanding—and ultimately seizing—control of much of the Republican party machinery, eventually giving rise to Jacksonian democracy.

Today, both parties fear the potential consequences of mobilization. Republicans are concerned that it might lead to an influx of poor and minority voters unlikely to support the GOP. Some Republican conservatives, moreover, think that many ordinary Americans have fallen prey to a moral and intellectual weakness that renders them unfit to participate in government. Versions of this notion were put forward to explain why most Americans seemed unwilling to support the GOP's campaign to impeach President Clinton.[21]

As for the Democrats, although expansion of the electorate might benefit the party as a whole, an influx of tens of millions of new voters would represent a substantial risk for current officeholders at the national, state, and local levels. Even if these new voters remained loyal to the Democratic party as an institution, they might not support the party's current leadership. Moreover, various liberal interests allied with the Democrats, such as upper-middle-class environmentalists, public-interest lawyers, anti-smoking activists, and the like, could not be confident of retaining their influence in a more fully mobilized electoral environment.[22] Though it is seldom openly admitted, some liberal intellectuals and activists have little interest in increasing participation among working-class and lower-middle-class whites, whom they see as opponents of abortion rights and proponents of school prayer and unrestricted handgun ownership.[23]

Almost all American politicians purport to deplore the nation's low levels of voter turnout. Yet even modest efforts to boost turnout inspire little support in Washington and most state capitals. For example, most Republicans bitterly opposed the so-called Motor Voter Act, signed into law by President Clinton in 1993.[24] Congressional Democrats, for their part, were willing to delete those portions of the bill most likely to maximize registration among the poor, such as the provision for automatic registration for all clients at welfare offices. In fact, many Democrats had actually been happy to see President Bush veto a previous version of Motor Voter in 1992. At any rate, the Motor Voter Act has had little effect upon the size or composition of the electorate. Few of the persons registered under the act have actually voted. In 1996, the percentage of newly registered voters who appeared at the polls actually dropped.[25] Voter mobilization requires more than the distribution of forms. To bring tens of millions of new voters to the polls, political parties and candidates would have to engage in old-fashioned door-to-door electioneering, and this is a task they seem unwilling to undertake.

POLLING AND THE VIRTUAL CITIZEN

There is one way in which these now superfluous citizens do seem to play a day-to-day role in the political process, and that is through the ubiquitous practice of opinion polling. Citizens are constantly asked their views, and the press trumpets the results of these polls as if they had great significance. Politicians, interest groups, and government officials are eager to gauge public sentiment on issues ranging from abortion to zootomy. Some pollsters have argued that precisely because opinion surveys capture the views of those who do not participate, they provide a more accurate picture of public opinion than voting, group politics, or any other form of actual political activity. In his famous book *The Pulse of Democracy*, George Gallup, one of the founders of the modern polling industry, asserted that more than any other institution, opinion polls "bridge the gap between the people and those responsible for making decisions in their name."[26]

Of course, the reality is that polling has no formal impact upon government and politics. The Constitution does not require public officials to adhere to Gallup or even CBS/New York Times poll results. Note that during the entire Clinton impeachment process the President's poll standing remained high, as did Richard Nixon's.

Polling is so pervasive in contemporary America that "poll results" and "public opinion" are used as synonyms. But they are not synonymous. Public opinion can be articulated in ways that present a very different picture of popular views than the results of sample surveys.[27] Among these are: statements from leaders of interest groups, trade unions, and religious groups about their adherents' feelings; the hundreds of thousands of letters written each year to newspaper editors and to members of

Congress; and protests, riots, and demonstrations. Government officials often take note of all these symptoms of the public's mood. And of course before the invention of polling, as Chester Bernard once noted, legislators "read the local newspapers, toured their districts and talked with voters, received letters from the home state, and entertained delegations which claimed to speak for large and important blocks of voters."[28]

These alternative modes of gauging public opinion continue to be available. Yet when poll results differ from other interpretations of public opinion, the polls are almost certain to be presumed accurate. The labor leader whose account of the views of the rank and file differs from poll findings, or the politician who quarrels with a poll's assessment of the popularity of his positions, is immediately derided by the press. For example, in 1999 Republican congressional leaders claimed that public opinion as evidenced by letters and phone calls supported their efforts to impeach and convict President Bill Clinton, while national opinion polls indicated that the public opposed Clinton's removal from office. Virtually every commentator took the polls to be correct and accused Republicans of disregarding true popular sentiment.

This presumption in favor of the accuracy of opinion polls stems from their appearance of neutrality. Survey research is modeled after the methodology of the natural sciences and conveys an impression of technical sophistication and objectivity.[29] The polls, moreover, can claim to offer a more reliable and representative view of popular opinion than any alternative source of information. Individuals claiming to speak for groups sometimes speak only for themselves. The distribution of opinion reflected by letters to newspapers and government officials is notoriously biased. Demonstrators are always a tiny and unrepresentative segment of the populace. Indeed, by offering a more representative and objective picture of public opinion, the polls can refute false claims and biased representations of popular sentiment.

Nevertheless, polling does more than merely offer a scientific measure of public sentiment. It also profoundly affects the character of what is perceived to be public opinion. Polling is what statisticians call an "obtrusive measure."[30] Surveys do not simply measure continuities and changes in a naturally occurring phenomenon. They also define how individual opinions are to be aggregated and cumulated, as well as the topics upon which opinions will be expressed. The data reported by the polls should therefore be seen as the product of an interplay between opinion and the survey instrument rather than some pure and unadulterated description of the public's views. As they measure, surveys interact with opinion, producing important changes in the character and identity of the expressed views.

Subsidizing Opinion Assertion

Polling changes the character of public opinion in at least three important ways.[31] First, it subsidizes the cost of asserting opinions. In the absence of polling, those who hold an opinion must bear the cost and effort required to organize and publicly communicate that opinion. Someone wishing to express a view about abortion, for example, might write a letter, deliver a speech, contribute to an organization, or attend a rally. Whatever the means chosen, the public communication of opinion entails an expenditure of time, energy, and perhaps money. Polls, by contrast, organize and publicize opinion without requiring any individual action. Indeed, hardly any of those whose views are nominally captured in a survey are actually even interviewed. A survey purporting to reflect the opinions of 250 million Americans is typically based upon interviews with only two or three thousand randomly sampled respondents.[32] The remainder are statistically or "virtually" represented.

This displacement of costs from the opinion-holder to the polling agency affects the character of the opinions likely to be expressed. In general, the willingness of individuals to bear the costs of publicly asserting their views is closely tied to the intensity with which they hold those views. There is unlikely to be a march on the Capitol by, for example, groups wishing to assert that they are indifferent toward abortion. Moreover, persons with strongly held views on a given question are also more likely to be found at the extremes of opinion.[33] As long as the costs of asserting opinions are borne by opinion-holders themselves, those with intense—often relatively extreme—views are disproportionately likely to be heard in the public forum.

Polls undermine this relationship between public expression and the intensity of opinion. The views of those who care little about a given issue are as likely to be publicized as the views of those who care a great deal about it. For this reason, the opinion reported in surveys is typically both less intense and less extreme than the opinion that might be voluntarily asserted by those with an active interest in the issue.[34] Polls, in effect, submerge individuals with strongly held views in a less interested mass public.

This submergence has both positive and negative implications. On the one hand, the polls are likely to dispel claims of public support by small groups of radicals or politicians at the ideological fringes. For example, despite Pat Buchanan's claims to speak for "brigades" of true conservatives in 1996 and 2000, surveys indicated that the isolationist views of this right-wing political commentator and perennial presidential candidate had the support of barely 2 per cent of the American people.

At the same time, however, the polls can also allow governments and politicians to claim that their policies or programs are consistent with public opinion even in the face of manifest public discontent. President Richard Nixon claimed to be governing on behalf of the "silent majority" of Americans who did not join protest marches or picket lines to demand changes in American race relations and an end to the Vietnam war, and who, according to the polls, did not even have strong views on the issues. With its "silent majority" notion, the administration used poll data to undermine the political weight and credibility of the hundreds of thousands of Americans who *did* feel strongly about race relations and Vietnam. The administration preferred to govern on behalf of this silent majority precisely because of its silence; its opinions imposed no constraint upon the government's conduct. In a sense, opinion polls came to be used *against* those who truly had opinions.

From Collective to Individual Opinion

A second way in which polling transforms opinion is to change it from a property of groups into an attribute of individuals. Prior to the advent of polling, information about the attitudes of ordinary Americans often came from the leaders of organized groups. Those interested in the views of working people, for example, might consult trade-union officials. To learn the attitudes of farmers one might turn to the heads of farm organizations. The claims of these leaders to have special knowledge of their members' views enhanced their own influence in political affairs and also increased the political weight of the groups they led. Because the leader spoke for the group as a unified entity, the forces with which the group interacted were likely to regard it as such.

By contrast, opinion surveys elicit the views of individuals directly. There is no need to rely upon group leaders for such information. Polling is likely to expose the fact that the members of any given group will almost inevitably disagree with one another and with their nominal leaders on many issues. This, too, has both positive and negative consequences. On the positive side, survey data may prevent the leaders of a group from accidentally or deliberately misrepresenting their members' views. For example, the views of delegates to political conventions differ considerably from those of the average voter. Republican delegates tend to be much more conservative than GOP voters, while Democratic delegates are decidedly more liberal than typical Democrats. The polls are a helpful reminder to party leaders that, for instance, not all Democrats would support the views articulated at the August 2000 convention by gay-rights activists,[35] nor do all Republicans share the beliefs of leaders of the party's religious right.

But at the same time, the polls can undermine a group's influence in the political process by refuting the claims of group leaders and activists to speak for their members. For example, during the 1950s organized labor bitterly opposed the Taft-Hartley Act, which union leaders dubbed a "slave-labor act." After President Truman vetoed it, the presidents of major unions vowed to work for the defeat of any member of Congress who voted to override Truman's veto. But while senators and representatives weighed their options, poll data showed that most union members neither fully understood the Taft-Hartley Act nor saw it as the factor that would determine their choice at the polls. These findings emboldened a number of legislators with large trade-union constituencies to vote for the bill, and Truman's veto was overridden.[36]

Interestingly, in the nineteenth and early twentieth centuries, political polling was introduced in the United States by such upper-class forces as the Mugwumps and Progressives as a way of reducing the collective power of their working-class opponents, who depended heavily upon disciplined organizations to make up for their members' individual lack of resources and influence.[37] The conservative *Chicago Tribune* was a major sponsor of polls in the 1890s, while the Hearst newspapers were avid promoters of polling in the early twentieth century. Today, of course, all political forces make extensive use of polling. But the fact remains that polling reduces the political weight of precisely those groups whose most important resource is the collective weight of their opinion.

From Spontaneous to Constrained Opinion

Third, polling transforms popular opinion from a spontaneous assertion to a constrained response. In the absence of polling, individuals choose the topics upon which to express their views. Someone who takes the trouble to submit a letter to a newspaper generally writes on a topic of his or her own choosing. The organizers of a protest march define the purpose of their action. But polling elicits views on topics selected by the survey's sponsors rather than by the respondents themselves. Publicly expressed opinion becomes less an assertion of individuals' own concerns and more a response to the concerns of others.

The most obvious consequence of this change is that polling can create a misleading impression of the agenda of public concerns. For example, during August 2000, daily polls indicated enormous swings in the relative standing of candidates Al Gore and George W. Bush. On August 7, the USA Today/CNN poll showed Bush leading Gore by nineteen points. On August 8, Bush's lead had dropped to two points in the same poll. Four days later, his lead was back up to ten points.[38] One fact never mentioned by these polls was that for most Americans the choice between Bush and Gore had not (or at least not yet) become important, and so respondents did not have firm opinions. The candidates' standing was very important to the pollsters but not to the public.

Given the commercial character of the polling industry, differences between the polls' concerns and those of the general public are probably inevitable. Polls generally raise questions that are of interest to purchasers of poll data—newspapers, political candidates, government agencies, business corporations. These questions may or may not reflect citizens' own needs and hopes. Perhaps more important, most poll questions have as their ultimate purpose some form of exhortation. Corporations poll to determine how best to persuade customers to purchase their wares. Candidates poll to find out how to convince voters to support them. Governments poll to learn how to ensure popular cooperation, or, as the National Performance Review might put it, to create less troublesome customers. In essence, rather than offering those in power the opinions that the citizens want them to learn, polls tell them what they would like to learn about citizens' opinions. The end result is to change the public expression of opinion from an assertion of demand to a step in the process of persuasion. In essence, the polls serve as tools for the management of opinion.

POLLING AND PUBLIC MANAGEMENT

This use of surveys is one element in the larger transformation of democratic government into a form of public management and of citizens into customers. This new perspective emerges in the public-administration literature that teaches government executives how to view the citizens they nominally serve and in the 1993 Report of the National Performance Review, the manifesto of the Clinton administration's campaign to "reinvent" government.

Traditionally, teachers and scholars of public administration emphasized the principle of democratic responsibility. Administrators were expected to remember that their agencies ultimately were responsible to the public and its elected representatives. Fritz Morstein Marx ably summarized the traditional scholarly injunction to administrators: "Public responsibility . . . asserts the necessity of providing demonstrable public benefits and of meeting public expectations. . . . Public responsibility under popular government further demands the willing subjection of the bureaucracy to the laws as the general instruction of the representatives of the people."[39]

These traditional strictures stand in sharp contrast to the guidance given by a widely used contemporary public-administration text. The authors of this text regard the public as an entity to be "managed" by a successful administrator rather than the ultimate source of authority in the political community. They give this advice to administrators:

> You should work hard to cultivate outside group support for your mission. . . . When you deal with the general public you should expect its members to have a limited understanding of the complexity of most issues. . . . While it is to your advantage to have the public on your side, this may not always be possible. Your organization may have a mission that is in conflict with . . . community groups. . . . Your job is to uphold your organization's mission. . . . Be prepared to suffer through public outcries, insults and demonstrations while supporting your program goals.[40]

The book, typical of contemporary public-administration texts, goes on to offer advice on how to manage the media, representative institutions, community groups, and the public at large. In essence, the new administrative training has substituted manipulation of the public for accountability to the public. This shift is reflected in the "reinvention of government" literature of the 1990s and in the report of the National Performance Review (NPR) commissioned by the Clinton administration under Vice President Al Gore's supervision in 1993.[41] The NPR is, of course, only the most recent example of a commission on government organization created by a president hoping to reform the federal bureaucracy in a way that would provide him with political advantages. Other examples include the New Deal–era Brownlow Committee, the Hoover commissions of the 1940s and 1950s, and the Ash Council created by Richard Nixon, who hoped to find an administrative formula that would give him greater control over the federal bureaucracy.[42] These earlier reorganization commissions assumed that public accountability and responsibility were central tenets of public administration. For example, the First Hoover Commission report began with its chair's observation that "the President, and under him his chief lieutenants, the department heads, must be held responsible and accountable to the people and the Congress for the conduct of the executive branch."[43]

This sentiment must have seemed a given if not a cliché to the authors of the Hoover report. Yet it stands in sharp contrast to the tone of the recent NPR report, which, as James Q. Wilson has observed, fails even to mention democratic accountability.[44] Indeed, the NPR report generally fails to use the term "citizens." In its preamble to chapter 2, "Putting Customers First," the report quotes Vice President Gore as saying, "A lot of people don't realize that the federal government has customers. We have customers. The American people."[45] *Citizens* were thought to own the government. *Customers*, by contrast, are merely expected to receive pleasant service from it. Citizens are members of a political community with a collective existence created for public purposes. Customers are individual purchasers seeking to meet their private needs in a market. What is missing from the experience of customers is mobilization to achieve collective interests, and the omission is not just a matter of changing semantic fashions along the Potomac.

In keeping with a customer-friendly orientation, government employees are advised to be courteous and more "user-friendly" at all times. Agencies are admonished to provide friendly surroundings for customers and to conduct frequent customer-satisfaction surveys. But the report has little or nothing to say about how customers might actually influence the substance of federal programs and their administration.[46] The notion that government agencies are ultimately accountable to ordinary people appears to be fading from sight.

At the end of the eighteenth century, America was the first nation with a mass electorate. In the middle of the nineteenth century, America was the first nation with strong mass-based political parties. At the end of the twentieth century, America became the first nation with a virtual citizenry. To be sure, millions of Americans not only continue to vote but also have unprecedented opportunities for political access through the media, the bureaucracy, and the courts. The American upper-middle class practices what we have called personal democracy with great effect. Tens of millions of other Americans, however, live outside this political sphere. Their presence in the political process is increasingly a statistical matter of virtual representation through polling.

The views of these virtual citizens, so carefully monitored by the polls, have been robbed of the qualities that once made public opinion an important phenomenon. Those with strong views are submerged among the apathetic. Groups and collectivities are atomized, and their political weight reduced. And, finally, consistent with their status as customers, they are polled so that they will become more amenable to persuasion. Confined to the political margins, these virtual citizens can watch political processes and struggles in which they are not invited to participate.

Response:
Refined and Enlarged Public Opinion

Benjamin I. Page

Most modern advocates of democracy accept James Madison's idea that government policy should reflect only the "refined" and "enlarged" opinions of the citizenry. That is, governments should not mechanically respond to whatever top-of-the-head views the average citizen might initially offer when he or she first hears about a given policy issue. Instead, policymaking should take account of opinion that results from careful thought and discussion and incorporates the best available information and expertise. That is to say, most modern advocates of democracy favor some sort of *deliberative* democracy.

As I see it, many disagreements about the proper role of public opinion and opinion surveys in a democratic polity flow from disagreements concerning exactly *who* should deliberate, under what circumstances. To put it another way, the crucial disagreements concern exactly *how* opinion is—or can be—refined and enlarged, and exactly *who* does or should do the refining and enlarging.

Those who uphold indirect, representative democracy, for example, including the Founders of the U.S. Constitution and their contemporary followers, want the refining and enlarging of public opinion to be done by elected or appointed representatives of the people. Such representatives, it is hoped, will deliberate on complex issues of public policy with a higher level of skill, experience, and expertise, and will devote to

Benjamin I. Page is Gordon S. Fulcher Professor of Decision-Making in the political science department at Northwestern University. He is author of seven books, including *The Rational Public: Fifty Years of Trends in Americans' Policy Preferences* (with Robert Shapiro), and *Who Deliberates? Mass Media in Modern Democracy*.

82

deliberation much more time and attention than the average citizen possibly can. In addition, representatives may be less subject to self-interested passions and less swayed by demagogues or manipulators. So long as such representatives are *accountable* to the general public, one argument goes, they will work on behalf of the true interests and values of the citizenry. They will enact just the sorts of public policies that the average citizen *would* enact if he or she had time to learn all the relevant facts and to deliberate thoroughly about how best to pursue the public interest.

Other observers, too, including James Fishkin, are concerned that the average citizen, consumed by daily tasks, may not have the time or inclination to deliberate thoroughly about public policy and may be misled by demagogues. But Fishkin is uneasy about delegating the task of deliberation wholly to official representatives. This unease apparently arises mainly from a concern that official "representatives" may not always represent properly. Differing in many ways from the average citizen (generally being much more affluent, for example), they may pursue class interests or selfish interests of their own. Or—given pervasive political inequalities in the electoral system—representatives may respond to the wishes of well-organized or moneyed groups that can help get them elected and re-elected, rather than to the interest of the public as a whole. Instead of relying on officially elected or appointed representatives, Fishkin advocates specially convened *deliberative assemblies*, consisting of statistically representative samples of citizens who are enabled to take time off from daily life, study relevant factual material, hear from experts, and deliberate about policy. After such deliberation, *deliberative opinion polls* ascertain the newly refined and enlarged views of these citizens, which can be taken as an indicator of what the citizenry as a whole would think after equivalent deliberation. Thus deliberative polls are intended to provide a guide to democratic policymaking.

Still other observers, including Benjamin Barber, take Fishkin's logic one step further. They distrust official representatives but are hesitant about special deliberative assemblies as well. In such assemblies, they ask, who gets to decide exactly *which* experts and *which* "objective facts" are presented to the sample of citizens? Which policy alternatives are taken seriously: only an official "two sides"? Won't choices about these matters tend to reflect the biases of the forum organizers, or of political elites in the broader society? (In Fishkin's Australian forum, what part was played by members of Parliament who favored indirect rather than direct election of a president?) Advocates of participatory democracy would like *all* citizens—or as many citizens as possible—to take an active part in political deliberation. Some also favor direct policymaking by ordinary citizens, through town meetings and perhaps through initiatives and referendums.

Robert Shapiro and I take yet another view. We maintain that citizens' opinions about policy issues are often *already* refined and enlarged, in natural settings, through what we call *public* or *collective deliberation*. Facts, ideas, and expertise relevant to public policy circulate through the mass media; citizens observe the opinions and reasoning of trusted public figures; they discuss politics with friends, family, and co-workers. Our evidence from hundreds of surveys conducted over fifty years indicates that collectively, over time, citizens can and do form opinions that are generally stable, coherent, internally consistent, responsive to the available information, and sensible. And these opinions *can* be well measured by polls and surveys. We merely need to ignore egregiously bad polls of the sort that Benjamin Ginsberg cites, pay attention to good poll data (inferring trends only from changed answers to identical questions, for example), and insist that survey questions reflect the concerns of the public, not just elites.

Shapiro and I take the point that most of the actual making of public policy is best delegated to elected representatives who can develop expertise and spend time working out policy details. But we are skeptical that official representatives always pursue the public interest. We see citizens themselves as best able to ascertain their own interests and the interest of the public as a whole. While acknowledging that collective deliberation is sometimes flawed—it can and should be improved, particularly by improving the quality and diversity of voices conveyed by the mass media—we believe that it generally works rather well. At least it works well enough to render largely unnecessary any special deliberative assemblies or deliberative opinion polls, which often come up with about the same results, or—when they do not—may reflect the inculcation of biased information.

It is worthwhile to encourage more extensive political deliberation by all citizens. But most people have many things to do other than reading the *Congressional Record* or attending political meetings. Some degree of division of labor is appropriate in deliberation (e.g., through the media-disseminated voices of experts and commentators) as well as in policymaking.

It should be clear, from this outline of alternative positions, that the differences among them largely rest upon empirical disagreements concerning such matters as what factors have how much influence upon the selection and the behavior of policymakers; how public opinion is formed and what its characteristics are; how well or badly polls measure public opinion; exactly what goes on in Fishkin-style deliberative assemblies; and how well participatory democracy works or could be made to work. For example, if Fishkin's deliberative assemblies worked exactly as their advocates hope, and if official representative bodies like the U.S. Congress did so, too, the results of both should be virtually identical. Then we could, with serene indifference, entirely dispense with one or the other. Much depends on how they actually work.

I cannot in this brief space review the vast scholarly literature relevant to the central empirical questions. Instead I will simply highlight certain assessments of the evidence that underlie my own position. Some of these points are elaborated in other writings of mine, including *The Rational Public, Who Deliberates?,* and (particularly concerning political inequality) *What Government Can Do.*

▪ Studies of interest-group influence and of the role of money in elections and policymaking convince me that official elected representatives cannot always be relied upon to act in the interest of the general public. Political inequality is a major problem for American democracy.

▪ Studies of political attitudes and behavior indicate that efforts to get most or all members of the U.S. public to pay close attention to politics, to acquire expertise, and to deliberate about the details of public policy are likely to achieve only limited success.

▪ Studies of the mass media show that there are flaws in the political information that is conveyed to the public, including some systematic biases that deserve serious attention.

▪ Nonetheless, there is usually sufficient diversity and competition among information sources that the average citizen—with assistance from trusted public figures and personal acquaintances—can often arrive at policy opinions that faithfully reflect his or her own values and interests in light of the best available information.

▪ The process of measuring and aggregating individuals' policy preferences through properly designed opinion surveys tends to reduce the noise and uncertainty surrounding individuals' opinions, revealing *collective* policy preferences that are generally stable, coherent, consistent, and reflective of the best publicly available information.

■ Given the nature of public opinion as revealed by sample surveys, such polls and surveys—when properly designed and interpreted—can appropriately be used as a guide to democratic policymaking. There is generally no need for recourse to special deliberative polls, which are more expensive to conduct, seldom yield very different results, and have a problematic normative status.

I do not want to convey a sense of utter complacency. On some technical matters and in early stages on some issues, public opinion may be meaningless or even nonexistent. Even on big, salient issues there are times when poll-measured public opinion evidently rests upon mistaken factual assumptions. Most Americans, for example, tend to overestimate government spending on foreign aid and underestimate spending on defense; few realize that earnings over about $76,000 are not subject to the Social Security payroll tax or that removal of this "cap" would solve most of the projected shortfall problem. In such cases, the public's expressed policy preferences may well deviate from what fully informed citizens would want.

In my view, however, when the public is misled it is generally the fault of information provided by elites (sometimes through governmental monopoly of foreign-affairs information, or two-party dominance of the political agenda) and transmitted through the mass media. In such cases I would like to see remedies directed at the system by which information is provided to the public. Rather than trying to bypass this system by ignoring tainted public opinion and consulting special deliberative assemblies, why not work to provide better information to the public as a whole?

Again, however, I believe that for the most part the public opinion routinely measured by polls and surveys is already sufficiently based on sound information, already sufficiently refined and enlarged, to serve as an appropriate guide to policymaking.

CHAPTER SIX

For the People:
Direct Democracy in the
State Constitutional Tradition

G. Alan Tarr

Two interrelated developments during the last quarter of the twentieth century bear directly on the theme of direct democracy. The first is the increased reliance on the initiative in the American states. From 1950 to 1974, states adopted only 279 initiatives, but in the succeeding twenty-five years they adopted 929.[1] This pronounced increase is not attributable to an increase in the number of states using the device: since 1975, only Mississippi has amended its constitution to authorize the constitutional initiative, and by the end of the century it had considered only two such initiatives, neither of which was adopted. Instead, the increase reflects a new—or, I would argue, renewed—willingness to circumvent established institutions of government that are perceived as unresponsive to the popular will. Some commentators trace this new constitutional populism to California's adoption in 1978 of Proposition 13, which froze property tax rates. But although Proposition 13 may have demonstrated the potential of the constitutional initiative and spawned analogous restrictions in other states, it was more a symptom than a cause.

G. Alan Tarr is director of the Center for State Constitutional Studies and Distinguished Professor of Political Science at Rutgers University. He is the author of *Understanding State Constitutions* and of *Judicial Process and Judicial Policymaking*, and he serves as the editor of *State Constitutions of the United States*, a fifty-two-volume reference series.

Related to this growth of constitutional populism has been an increase in the number and fervor of attacks on the initiative and on other forms of direct democracy.[2] To a considerable extent, these attacks echo complaints about direct democracy voiced originally by opponents of the Progressives during the early years of the twentieth century, an ironic twist since many of those criticizing the initiative today define their political stance as progressive. (Not all the recent criticism repeats earlier complaints—consider, for example, the oft-repeated claim that initiatives have exacerbated divisions along the lines of race, ethnicity, and sexual orientation.) In this essay I will focus on a common and long-standing argument against direct democracy, what might be called the "if Madison could see this, he would roll over in his grave" argument.

According to this argument, the omission of mechanisms for direct democracy from the United States Constitution was neither accident nor oversight but rather a conscious choice on the part of the Founders. Joseph Bessette has elegantly summarized this perspective in his excellent book on deliberation in Congress.[3] According to Bessette, the Founders believed that a properly designed system of representative government would be more likely to be guided by the "cool and deliberate sense of the community" than would a direct democracy, and so the "public voice, pronounced by the representatives of the people, [would] be more consonant to the public good than if pronounced by the people themselves, convened for that purpose." The key phrase is "properly designed," for the way in which legislatures are constructed affects both the relations between representatives and their constituents and the dynamics within the legislative bodies. By creating large congressional districts, the Founders sought to prevent the election of local demagogues and to place governmental power in the hands of persons of stature, who would be able to discern the interests of the citizenry and the best means of serving those interests. In addition, large districts meant that the legislature would be relatively small, and this would facilitate reasoned deliberation. By giving representatives an extended term of office, the Founders guaranteed them the independence needed to oppose the "temporary delusion[s]" of the populace. Their extended tenure also would enable them to gain the knowledge and experience necessary to legislate wisely. In sum, the Founders believed that a system promoting deliberation by experienced and knowledgeable representatives would tend to "refine and enlarge the public views"; it would therefore be more likely to serve "the permanent and aggregate interests of the community" than would a system of direct popular rule.[4]

I have no quarrel with Bessette's depiction of the views of the architects of the federal Constitution—perhaps Madison *is* turning over in his grave at the increase in direct democracy. I do object to the whiff of nativism that occasionally accompanies the "rolling over in his grave" argument: the insinuation that the initiative should be rejected because it is an unsuitable import from a country previously famous only for army knives and cheese fondue. But my more serious objection is to the oft-repeated claim that the views of Madison and other framers of the federal Constitution are authoritative because they represent *the* American constitutional tradition. The United States has not one constitution but fifty-one. These constitutions were drafted at various stages in the nation's history, and they reflect the constitutional thought regnant in their day. The political theory underlying state constitutions often diverged from the perspective of 1787. In fact, some state constitution-makers expressly repudiated the handiwork of James Madison and his compatriots. A delegate to the Nevada convention of 1864, for example, attacked the "profound and reverential regard which some profess for the men who assembled in the early years of the republic, *when the government was yet but an experiment*," and a California delegate in 1878 insisted that there was nothing to be gained by looking at constitutions formed in such "primitive times." Even eighteenth-century state constitutions reflected a distinctive perspective on republican government and its problems—otherwise, Madison would not have spent so much time criticizing these constitutions at the Constitutional Convention and in the *Federalist Papers*.

This all suggests that there is a distinct state constitutional tradition, one that differs in significant respects from the federal constitutional tradition.[5] In delineating the relation of direct democracy to this state tradition, I will advance three claims:

▪ First, the initiative—and direct democracy more generally—fits comfortably within the state constitutional tradition.

▪ Second, this compatibility derives from the belief, basic to the state constitutional tradition, that the primary danger facing republican government is minority faction—power wielded by the wealthy or well-connected few—rather than majority faction.

▪ Third, divergence of the state tradition from the diagnosis in *Federalist* 10 of the threats to republican government is paralleled by a skepticism about the "republican remedies" proposed in the *Federalist Papers*.

More specifically, the state constitutional tradition is characterized by a distrust of government by elected representatives: representation fails to solve the problems afflicting republican government and may even aggravate those problems by empowering minority factions. If this is so, of course, then direct democracy—or mechanisms designed to approximate it—becomes much more attractive.

State Constitutionalism in the 18th Century

Direct popular participation in the making and revising of constitu-tions has been a feature of state constitutionalism from the very outset. The declarations of rights in the initial state constitutions consistently acknowledged that "all political power is vested in and derived from the people only" and that the people consequently have "an incontestable, unalienable, and indefeasible right" to "reform, alter, or totally change [government] when their protection, safety, prosperity, and happiness require it" (Va. Declaration of Rights, sec. 3).[6] By the 1830s the mechanism for obtaining direct popular approval had become standardized: referendums on whether to hold constitutional conventions and on whether to ratify proposed constitutional revisions and amendments. Prior to that, the states experimented with other means of assessing public support for constitutional innovations, including (in Maryland, North Carolina, and Pennsylvania) distributing copies of the draft document among the citizenry. Tapping public sentiment, giving state citizens a chance to participate directly, was viewed as perfectly natural and indeed obligatory.

State constitutions of the eighteenth and early nineteenth centuries tended to concentrate power for the day-to-day operation of government in the legislature. In addition to enacting laws and imposing taxes, the legislatures in most states selected the governor and state judges and appointed other state officials (and often local officials as well). Legislators could remove officials by impeachment and require the removal of judges. Moreover, these broad powers existed virtually without check, for most governors lacked the veto as well as an independent political base, judicial review was as yet undeveloped, and state constitutions imposed few restrictions beyond those enshrined in declarations of rights.

Why would state constitution-makers lodge such power in a single institution, particularly if they were skeptical of representative government? In part, the answer is that the legislature was the only institution that directly represented the citizenry. Even more important, however, was the relationship between representative and constituents envisioned by state constitutions, which differed dramatically from that sketched in the *Federalist Papers*. To put it simply, state constitution-makers sought to approximate direct democracy in their systems of representative government.

State Constitutions and Representation

The radical Pennsylvania constitution of 1776, later copied by Vermont, illustrates clearly how this might be done. This constitution vested broad power in a popularly elected unicameral legislature, granting it— in addition to the specifically granted powers—"all other powers necessary for the legislature of a free state or commonwealth" (sec. 9). The legislature was large, with small electoral districts that not only facilitated close contact between legislators and their constituents but also made it more likely that representatives would mirror demographically the people they represented. The constitution apportioned the legislature on the basis of the number of taxable inhabitants, which was said to be "the only principle which can . . . make *the voice of a majority of the people the law of the land*" (sec. 17, italics added). Annual election kept legislators on a tight rein, and a constitutionally prescribed rotation in office served to avoid "the danger of establishing an inconvenient aristocracy" (sec. 19). Finally, the Pennsylvania constitution wove various plebiscitary elements into the fabric of government. It enforced popular control over lawmaking by imposing a waiting period to allow for popular consideration of proposed legislation. Except "on occasions of sudden necessity," enactments did not take effect prior to the election of a new assembly. This gave voters an opportunity to install legislators pledged to repeal unpopular legislation. This, combined with the important right of the people to "instruct their representatives," served to reinforce the point that "the people of this State have the sole, exclusive, and inherent right of governing" and that "all officers of government . . . are their trustees and servants" (Pa. Declaration of Rights, arts. 16, 3, and 4).

The Pennsylvania constitution of 1776 was premised on the notion that representation was a necessary evil, acceptable only because distance and population size precluded the operation of direct democracy, and that the system of representative government should therefore replicate direct democracy insofar as possible. Representatives were to represent the views of the populace faithfully, rather than (as Madison recommended) refining and enlarging those views.

Neither Pennsylvania's effort to approximate direct democracy nor the devices it used to accomplish this end were unique. All but one of the original states kept members of the lower house of the state legislature on a tight rein through annual elections, and the sole exception, South Carolina, bowed to this consensus in 1778. By 1789 seven states had instituted annual elections for members of the upper house as well. Most states emulated Pennsylvania in establishing large lower houses, with the expectation that small electoral districts would link legislators closely with their constituents. Five state constitutions also followed Pennsylvania's in expressly authorizing the people to "instruct" their representatives, and the practice was widespread even in states that did not expressly recognize it in their constitutions. Virginia's Declaration of Rights summarized the prevailing understanding: "All power is vested in, and consequently derived from, the people; . . . magistrates are their trustees and servants, *and at all times amenable to them*" (sec. 2, italics added).

The Jury

No discussion of direct democracy during the late eighteenth and early nineteenth centuries would be complete without mention of the jury. Juries gave citizens the opportunity to participate directly in the administration of law, just as the instructing of representatives and the other mechanisms I have described gave them the opportunity to participate in its creation. Alexis de Tocqueville highlighted the close connection between these two forms of direct participation in governance, observing: "The jury system as understood in America seems to me as direct and extreme a consequence of the dogma of the sovereignty of the people as universal suffrage. They are . . . equally powerful means of making the majority prevail."[7] Thomas Jefferson went even further, insisting that if called upon to decide "whether the people had best be omitted in the legislative or judiciary departments," he "would say it is better to leave them out of the legislative," as "the execution of laws is more important than the making of them."[8]

One should underscore Tocqueville's phrase "as understood in America," because the role of the jury in America differed from that in

England in ways pertinent to discussions of direct democracy.[9] In England, a division of responsibility had developed, such that juries decided questions of fact and judges decided questions of law. But during the decades prior to the Revolution, juries in America came to be understood as having the authority to render judgment on matters of both fact and law. The jury served as a sort of lower house in the judicial branch, allowing the people to counter arbitrariness and lawlessness by judges, who after all lacked the institutional safeguards of independence. Even more important, the authority of jurors to determine the law stemmed from the democratic belief that ordinary citizens had as great an ability as judges to discern what the law was.

This understanding of the people's competence to participate directly in the administration of justice found expression in eighteenth-century state constitutions. In fact, the right to jury trial—what the New Jersey constitution called "the inestimable right of trial by jury" (art. 22)—was the only right guaranteed by all the original state constitutions. Even those constitutions without declarations of rights safeguarded the right to trial by jury. The language common to several of these provisions seemed to give juries the same broad authority they had exercised during the colonial era. The Pennsylvania constitution of 1776, for example, mandated that "trials shall be by jury *as heretofore*" (sec. 25, italics added). The Georgia constitution of 1777 was more explicit, saying that "the jury shall be judges of law as well as of fact" (art. 41).

The important point, then, is that all eighteenth-century state constitutions recognized and protected the jury as a form of direct popular participation in governing.

STATE CONSTITUTIONALISM IN THE 19TH CENTURY

By the 1830s, citizens in most states had concluded that their initial efforts to approximate direct democracy had failed. In particular, they believed that state legislators remained more responsive to the wealthy and well-connected than to the general public. This prompted a wave of constitutional reform. Fifteen of the twenty-four states that were in the Union by 1830 had revised their constitutions by 1860, and two of them had done so twice. Most state constitutions that developed during this period sought to secure the independence and autonomy of the executive and judicial branches as a vital step in the creation of a system of checks and balances. They did this by replacing legislative appointment of governors and other executive officials with popular election and, after 1846, extending popular election to judges as well.

The introduction of checks and balances might suggest that they were emulating the federal Constitution; but despite some surface similarities to the federal model, the state reforms were primarily concerned with preventing faithless legislators from frustrating the popular will, not with checking majority faction. The fact that executive officials and judges were directly elected was crucial. Popular election not only ensured accountability but also allowed executive officials and judges to claim that they had just as strong a connection to the people, the source of all political authority, as did legislators.

A delegate to the South Dakota constitutional convention of 1889 provided what might be seen as the motto of nineteenth-century constitution-makers: "The object of constitutions is to limit the legislature."[10] Few believed that checks and balances were sufficient to achieve that end. Distrust of elected representatives led states to impose various procedural requirements on the legislative process, ranging from mandating that all bills be referred to committee to requiring that bills embrace a single subject and that their titles accurately reflect their contents. These reforms served to increase the transparency of the legislative process, thereby facilitating popular control and deterring legislative misbehavior.

As the century progressed, constitutional restrictions on legislatures proliferated. Late nineteenth-century constitutions typically restricted the state legislature to biennial regular sessions and limited the length of those sessions. In fact, a delegate to the California convention of 1879 even proposed that "[t]here shall be no legislature convened from and after the adoption of this Constitution . . . and any person who shall be guilty of suggesting that a Legislature be held, shall be punished as a felon without benefit of clergy."[11] State constitutions also imposed numerous subject-matter restrictions on legislative action, seeking to combat special privilege and the threat of corruption by forbidding legislatures to enact special or local laws in various areas of public policy. The numbers speak for themselves: the Illinois constitution of 1870 prohibited the state legislature from addressing twenty fields of local or private concern, the Pennsylvania constitution of 1873 forty, and the California constitution of 1879 thirty-three.

Turning to the Convention

These efforts to rein in state legislatures did not signal an abandonment of the hope of approximating direct democracy. However, during the nineteenth century the locus of that hope shifted from state legislature to the constitutional convention. A delegate to the Illinois convention of 1847 expressed this new perspective: "We are what the people of the State would be, if they were congregated here in one mass meeting."[12] This shift in perspective set off a truly extraordinary burst of constitutional activity. Over the course of the century, the American states held 144 constitutional conventions and adopted ninety-four constitutions.[13]

Several factors recommended the constitutional convention as a mechanism for approximating direct democracy. First, the membership of such conventions tended to mirror the populace of the states. Like state legislators, convention delegates were elected by the people, but unlike legislators, most were not professional politicians. Although no comprehensive study of the backgrounds of convention delegates exists, the available evidence indicates that delegates tended to resemble their constituents quite closely.[14]

Second, the people exercised control over the calling of conventions. Whereas the legislature met regularly, a convention came into being only by popular vote, when the people wanted fundamental political issues addressed. Convention delegates therefore had a ready-made agenda of popular concerns to guide their deliberations. True, in most states the people could not vote to call a convention unless the state legislature first put a convention call on the ballot. But while this might seem to be a major impediment, in practice it did not turn out that way. Popular pressure could induce even reluctant legislators to schedule a vote on a convention, as happened in Virginia in 1829 and in Mississippi in 1832.

Furthermore, when legislators refused to bow to the popular will, citizens sometimes took matters into their own hands and convened extralegal conventions. They defended their actions in terms that emphasized the importance of direct popular rule, insisting that the people were simply exercising their "undubitable, unalienable, and indefeasible right to reform, alter, or abolish government" in order to promote the public good (Va. Declaration of Rights, art. 3). The most famous of these extralegal conventions occurred in Rhode Island in 1842 during the Dorr Rebellion and led to the landmark Supreme Court ruling in

Luther v. Borden.[15] Other states that held extralegal conventions during the nineteenth century include Maryland, Michigan, and Kansas.

Third, ratification by referendum afforded the people an opportunity to approve or reject the measures proposed by constitutional conventions—not an approximation of direct democracy but the real thing. State electorates did not simply rubber-stamp what conventions proposed. From 1877 to 1887, for example, voters in six states rejected proposed constitutions. Usually voters considered the proposed constitution as a whole rather than voting on particular provisions. Yet in some states the practice developed of submitting controversial proposals as separate items, lest opposition to them doom the entire document. In New York, for example, the convention of 1846 permitted a separate vote on a provision guaranteeing voting rights for blacks, and the convention of 1894 authorized separate votes on provisions dealing with apportionment and canals. This separate submission of provisions closely resembles the constitutional initiative.

The nineteenth-century faith in the constitutional convention as a close approximation of direct democracy led, as has the constitutional initiative, to a constitutionalization of policymaking. The convention was viewed as an opportunity to escape politics as usual, the politics of corruption and parochial advantage, and to replace it with a politics of the popular will and the public interest. Consequently, convention delegates inserted a great deal of legislation into the constitutions they wrote, seeking a penetration of the more pristine politics of constitution-making into the realm of legislation. Commenting on the phenomenon, James Bryce wrote that the delegates "neither wished nor cared to draw a line of distinction between what is proper for a constitution and what ought to be left to be dealt with by the state legislature."[16] But others took a different view. Governor Arthur Mellette eloquently presented the case for constitutional legislation at the South Dakota convention of 1889: "If you know what is the proper thing to embrace in your legislation, the more there is in the constitution the better *for the people*. . . . It is wise, in my judgment, after *the people* have decided in what direction their interests lie, to embody them in the fundamental law of the land and make it permanent."[17]

From the Convention to the Initiative

Whether state constitutional conventions during the nineteenth century in fact approximated direct democracy may be open to dispute (although it is interesting that many of those who today oppose calling a convention to amend the federal Constitution base their opposition on the worry that it would reflect public opinion all too well). Even if they did reflect public opinion, a convention is a rather blunt instrument for dealing with governmental institutions that are not responsive to the popular will. After all, a convention is an extraordinary intervention in the political process, while the problem it is seeking to address is an ongoing one. In any event, the idea of a constitutional convention as a mechanism for popular policymaking has faded. Instead, the movement has been toward streamlining constitutions. The number of state constitutional conventions has decreased dramatically since the nineteenth century, and the impetus for conventions has shifted from the populace to political elites. Indeed, state electorates in recent decades have become skeptical of the benefits of constitutional revision, rejecting several proposed constitutions and consistently rejecting convention calls in those states that mandate periodic votes on whether to hold a convention.

The decline of the constitutional convention led in the twentieth century to the emergence of the initiative as the preferred mechanism for ensuring that government reflect the popular will. Like the convention, the initiative is an effort to deal with the problem of unresponsive and unaccountable legislators. And like the convention, it attempts to make the popular will effectual by translating it directly into public policy. But unlike the convention, it seeks to give the people the opportunity to make policy on an ongoing basis rather than merely on extraordinary occasions. Of course, whether the initiative in fact empowers the populace remains a hotly contested question.

Concluding Observations

In the "Gettysburg Address," Abraham Lincoln spoke of "government of the people, by the people, and for the people." Both the long-standing efforts to approximate direct democracy and the current reliance on the constitutional initiative are rooted in a perception that even a system of government *of* and *by* the people may not produce a government *for* the people. Recent constitutional initiatives have directly addressed this concern. For example, imposing term limits seeks to weed out politicians who are more concerned with careerism than with the public good; fiscal restrictions are an effort to limit the damage that such politicians can do; and restrictions on pensions and other perks for public officials are meant to discourage anyone from pursuing public office out of material self-interest. Initiatives restricting state taxing and spending further serve the goal of a government responsive to the people rather than to special interests by limiting the resources that legislators can dispense as benefits to such interests. Finally, some initiatives—for example, those dealing with affirmative action, with the right to die, with nuclear power, and with the tobacco industry—address issues of broad public concern that legislators had refused to put on the public agenda, either out of a fear of taking stands on contentious issues or out of a desire to avoid antagonizing powerful special interests.

Concern about the lack of popular control over public officials has been a recurring theme in state constitutionalism. Efforts to deal with this endemic problem have varied over time, with new mechanisms tried when the old have proven ineffective. During the late eighteenth and early nineteenth centuries, the primary mechanism was concentration of power in the hands of the state legislature, the people's representatives, with annual election, the instructing of representatives, and other devices used to bind those representatives to their constituents' wishes. During the nineteenth century, constitutional bans on special legislation were designed to make it more difficult for legislators to serve special interests, and requirements promoting transparency in the legislative process were adopted to discourage legislative misconduct by making it easier to detect and punish such misconduct. Also during the nineteenth century, constitutional conventions justified their insertion of detailed policy provisions into state constitutions by arguing that it was better to have policy made by a body truly responsive to the people than by political institutions that were invariably infected by corruption and self-interest. The adoption of the initiative during the twentieth century and its increased use in the latter decades of that century thus represent a continuation of efforts to secure government both by and for the people. As such, they fit comfortably within the American constitutional tradition properly understood—that is, an understanding that encompasses constitutional thought and practice at both the federal and the state level.

I have argued that the initiative attempts to deal with the problem of unresponsive and unaccountable government, but I do not claim that it has succeeded. Many critics have charged that the initiative merely opens up a new arena for elite politics, in which special interests and wealthy or well-positioned policy entrepreneurs determine the constitutional agenda and manipulate the public. The evidence on this point is mixed. On the one hand, anecdotal evidence confirms that wealthy individuals and organizations have financed some ballot initiatives, and officials already influential in traditional political arenas have used initiatives to advance their policy agendas and, not coincidentally, their political careers. On the other hand, poll data reveal that those initiatives that have gained voter approval typically reflect popular views, even when turnout is less than optimal. The question, of course, is whether successful initiative campaigns tap deep-seated preexisting views or merely manufacture views.

In this essay I also do not claim that government policy that is more faithful to the unrefined views of the citizenry is a good thing, either in particular instances or in general. The argument of the *Federalist Papers* on the diseases most incident to republican government, even if drafted during what the California convention delegate dismissed as "primitive times," has certainly not been refuted. It may well be that one secures good government by being less simply democratic. Nevertheless, the history I have recounted here does indicate that the argument on the dangers of popular government has two sides, each with a claim to being an important part of the American constitutional tradition. It also suggests that the question cannot readily be resolved empirically, because none of the mechanisms that the states have employed to deal with the problem of minority faction has altogether succeeded, at least in the long run.

Philosophers have been said to be so fond of their questions that they are reluctant to see them definitively answered. But with the matter we have been considering here, I suspect that it is the sheer difficulty of the question, not a fondness for it, that will have us continuing to debate the desirability of direct democracy for a long time to come.

CHAPTER SEVEN

People Power:
Initiative and Referendum
in the United States

M. Dane Waters

Thomas Jefferson once said, "The people . . . are the only sure reliance for the preservation of our liberty." That simple statement summarizes not only Jefferson's belief but also the belief that this country was founded upon.

For a hundred years, the initiative and referendum process has been the critical tool to check the power of unresponsive and unaccountable government at the state and local level. Twenty-four states as well as countless cities and counties allow citizens to gather signatures on petitions to put a new law on the ballot for a public vote (the initiative process) or to refer a legislative act to the ballot for final voter approval (the referendum process). Governor William Janklow of South Dakota—the first state to adopt the initiative and referendum—had this to say about the process: "It is a tool of true democracy to allow citizens to participate directly in making the laws that affect their lives. People can define and decide the issue themselves if their elected officials aren't doing things to their satisfaction."

Initiative and referendum has existed in some form in this country

---

M. Dane Waters is the founder and president of the Initiative and Referendum Institute, Washington, D.C. He has written widely and lectured around the world on the importance of the initiative and referendum process. Previously he was the national field director of U.S. Term Limits, which is a non-partisan advocacy group.

since the 1600s. Citizens of New England placed ordinances and other issues on the agenda of forum meetings for discussion and then a vote. Thomas Jefferson proposed that the legislative referendum process be included in the 1775 Virginia constitution. The first state to hold a state-wide referendum for its citizens to ratify its constitution was Massachusetts in 1778. New Hampshire followed in 1792. Today, every state but Delaware requires a final vote of the people before the state constitution can be amended.

Jefferson was a strong advocate of the referendum process, which in his view recognized the people as sovereign. Whereas the King of England said that his power to govern was derived from God, Jefferson knew that those chosen to represent the citizenry in a republican form of government were empowered only by the people. This was the core principle upon which the federal Constitution was based.

State constitutions mirror the federal Constitution. In state constitutions, checks and balances were created to forestall the abuse of power by elected representatives and to protect the people from an out-of-control government. But people began to realize in the late 1800s that no matter what checks and balances existed, the people had no direct ability to affect an out-of-touch government or a government paralyzed by inaction. Then came the Populist Party of the 1890s. Its members were outraged at the idea that moneyed special-interest groups controlled government, and that the people had no ability to break this control. They soon began to propose a comprehensive platform of political reforms, including women's suffrage, secret ballots, direct election of U.S. senators, primary elections, and the initiative process.

The Populists believed that the initiative process was based on trust of the individual citizen. They wanted not to change the system of government but to enhance it. At both the federal and the state level there were splendid founding documents, but they were based on compromise. The Founders realized that constitutions would eventually need alteration, and they created mechanisms to change them when necessary. The system of checks and balances they devised was theoretical and unproven. As time went by, the citizens, led by the Populists and the Progressives, discovered that although this theoretical system of checks and balances worked, it didn't work well enough, for there were times when elected officials chose not to act in the people's best interest. The Populists and Progressives saw it as their duty to try to perfect the system of government so that it would accomplish the true intent of the Founders, which was to ensure that the people were the ultimate sovereign and that the government was there for the people, not the people for the government. They often quoted James Madison, who said in *Federalist* 49: "As the people are the only legitimate fountain of power, and it is from them that the constitutional charter, under which the several branches of government hold their power, is derived, it seems strictly consonant to the republican theory to recur to the same original authority . . . whenever it may be necessary to enlarge, diminish, or new-model the powers of the government."

Citizen use of the initiative process has a long and rich history in this country. Since the first statewide initiative on Oregon's ballot in 1904, citizens in the twenty-four states that have the initiative process have placed approximately 1,900 statewide measures on the ballot and have adopted 787 (41 per cent). In 1996, considered the high-water mark for the initiative process, citizens placed 102 measures on statewide ballots and adopted 45 (44 per cent). In contrast, the state legislatures that same year in those twenty-four states adopted more than 17,000 laws. Additionally, very few proposed initiatives actually make it to the ballot. In California, according to political scientist Dave McCuan, only 26 per cent of all initiatives filed have made the ballot and only 8 per cent of those filed actually were adopted by the voters. In 2000, more than 350 initiatives were filed in the twenty-four initiative states, and approximately 70 got on the ballot—about 20 per cent. A complete listing of initiatives since 1904, including some that will appear on future ballots, is available at www.iandrinstitute.org and www.ballotwatch.org.

Since 1904, when the first statewide initiative appeared, the initiative process has fluctuated greatly. From 1904 to 1976, use steadily declined from 291 in the decade 1911–1920 to only 78 in 1961–1970. The distraction of two world wars, the Great Depression, and the Korean War were largely responsible for the decline. However, with the passage in 1978 of California's Proposition 13, an initiative that cut state property taxes by nearly 60 per cent, the people began to realize the power of the process once again, and the two most prolific decades of initiative use have occurred since then: 1981–90, with 289 initiatives, and 1991–2000, with approximately 396. (See Table 1 on the following page.)

Even though 1991–2000 will go into the record books as the most prolific decade, with close to 400 initiatives making the ballot, it is uncertain what the future holds for the process. Public desire to use initiatives and referendums is high; poll after poll shows an average 70 per cent support for the process. But state legislatures have tried to rein in the use by imposing regulations and restrictions, such as a prohibition on signature collection at post offices. Citizens are therefore finding it much harder to use this important tool.

Table 1
STATEWIDE BALLOT INITIATIVES:
DECADES OF LEAST AND MOST USE

Decade	Number Proposed	Number Adopted	Passage Rate (%)
1941–1950	131	53	40
1951–1960	109	44	41
1961–1970	78	33	42
1991–2000 (est.)	396	194	48
1911–1920	291	117	40
1981–1990	289	127	44

One interesting note is that while twenty-four states have some form of statewide initiative, almost 60 per cent of initiative activity has taken place in just five states: Oregon, California, Colorado, North Dakota, and Arizona. Table 2 shows their usage.

Table 2
STATEWIDE BALLOT INITIATIVES:
STATES WITH MOST USE 1904–1998

State	Number Proposed	Number Adopted	Passage Rate (%)
Oregon	314	105	33
California	260	92	35
Colorado	174	72	41
North Dakota	165	77	47
Arizona	144	58	40

ACHIEVEMENTS OF THE INITIATIVE PROCESS

What has been accomplished through the use of this process? Some very fundamental things affecting our daily lives. Here are some examples of statewide reforms brought about by initiatives in various states:

Ended or outlawed:
- State funding of abortions
- Prohibition
- Use of racial preferences in government hiring and contracting
- Bi-lingual education
- Poll taxes
- The death penalty
- Use of steel traps in hunting

Legalized or required:
- Women's right to vote
- Eight-hour workday
- Prohibition
- Sale of yellow margarine
- Term limits for elected officials
- Direct primaries for election of officials
- Physician-assisted suicide
- Movie theater operation on Sunday
- Medical use of marijuana
- Bottle taxes for environmental protection
- Campaign finance reform
- The death penalty
- Parental notification before abortion
- Vote of the people on new tax increases
- Super-majority bicameral legislature vote to enact tax increases

These reforms represent various political agendas—conservative, liberal, libertarian and populist. This is typical of the initiative process—it can be used by persons of almost any political persuasion. Furthermore, the presence of an initiative on the ballot makes voters more likely to go to the polls. In election after election, voter turnout has been from 3 to 7 per cent higher in states with one or more initiatives on the ballot than in states without one. People believe that their vote can make a difference on an initiative. They realize that when an initiative they voted for passes, they get what they voted for, whether it was term limits, tax limits, educational or environmental reform, or something else. With a vote for a candidate there is no such guarantee.

The modern-day movement to utilize the initiative process can be said to have begun in 1978 in California, when the passage of Proposition 13 cut property taxes from 2.5 per cent of market value to just 1 per cent. Similar initiatives were subsequently adopted in Michigan and Massachusetts. Within two years, forty-three states had implemented some form of property-tax relief, and fifteen states had lowered their income-tax rates.

Another important reform that has come about through the initiative process is term limits on elected officials—what the Founders called "rotation in office." Eighteen state legislatures have been term-limited, all but one through an initiative. Term limits have also exploded on the scene at the local level—again, nearly always through the efforts of citizens who put the question directly to their fellow citizens. That's how activists in New York, Los Angeles, New Orleans, Denver, Kansas City, Houston, Nashville, Cincinnati, and many other cities have made term limits the law. Similarly, on the related issue of campaign finance, reformers around the country have bypassed state legislators, who obviously have a conflict of interest on the issue, and have taken reform measures directly to the people to enact.

THE TOP TEN INITIATIVE ISSUES IN 2000

Voters in the November 2000 election cast ballots for their choice for president of the United States, but also on a myriad of other subjects. More than 200 statewide ballot measures were certified for ballots in 42 states. Nearly a third were citizen-initiated measures, and the rest were legislative referendums. Here are the top ten issues:

1. Animal Protection: Initiatives were voted on in Massachusetts (banning dog racing), Montana (banning game farms), Oregon (banning traps and poisons), and Washington state (banning traps and poisons). Additionally, there was a popular referendum on the Alaska ballot on the legislature's attempt to allow hunters to use airplanes to land and shoot wolves on the same day. The animal-protection movement has had an impressive win record in recent years, primarily because of (a) the support of the Humane Society of the United States and (b) its growing expertise in using the initiative process. This time it won in Alaska, Montana, and Washington but lost in Massachusetts and Oregon.

2. Drug Policy: The biggest winner was the drug-policy reform movement. There were initiatives for allowing medical use of marijuana in Colorado and Nevada. Elsewhere the movement changed its focus to reforming asset-forfeiture laws and reforming sentencing policy for nonviolent drug offenders. Initiatives dealing with drug-policy reform passed in California (drug treatment), Colorado (medical marijuana), Nevada (medical marijuana), Oregon (asset-forfeiture reform) and Utah (asset-forfeiture reform). The only defeat was in Massachusetts (drug treatment). The legalizing of marijuana for recreational use, which was not part of the drug-policy reform efforts sponsored by international financier George Soros, was defeated in Alaska.

3. Education: There had never been a successful school-choice initiative, primarily because of the tremendous amount of time, energy, and money invested by the teachers' unions to fight these measures. School-choice advocates had hoped that 2000 would be the year when their efforts paid off. But it didn't happen. The anticipated "Goliath versus Goliath" fight—pitting the unions' millions against billionaire Tim Draper of California, Microsoft billionaire Paul Allen in Washington state, and the almost limitless purse of Amway founders Betsy and Dick DeVos in Michigan—was exactly that. The education-reform measures lost..

These results, coupled with initiative results in California (lower the threshold for passing local school bonds), Colorado (increase funding for public education), Oregon (increase funding for public education), and Washington state (increase teachers' pay and reduce class sizes), made it a good year for the advocates of public education, but not for school-choice advocates.

4. Guns: The NRA was largely silent on gun regulation this election cycle. Gun-control advocates had big victories in Colorado and Oregon with measures that will make purchasers of guns at gun shows subject to background checks. Because of these victories, there are certain to be other gun-control measures on ballots in the near future.

5. Health Care: Many people saw the defeat of universal health care in Massachusetts as a big defeat for the health-care reform movement, but in reality it was a victory. The mere fact that the measure was on the ballot served as the 800-pound gorilla that prompted the state legislature to pass a watered-down version of the measure. This has encouraged activists in other states to push for a similar reform in hopes that it will spur their legislators to act.

6. Physician-Assisted Suicide: In 1998, this issue had big victories in Oregon and a devastating loss in Michigan. The 2000 election dealt it another blow, when voters in Maine chose not to adopt a proposed death-with-dignity law.

7. Same-Sex Marriage/Gay Rights: Banning same sex-marriages was the new trend to watch at the ballot box. The issue was first tested in Hawaii and Alaska in 1998 and in California earlier in 2000. After these victories, opponents of same-sex marriage moved their focus inland, placing the issue on the ballots in Nebraska and Nevada. Both measures passed handily. Given these two victories, plus the failure of a measure in Maine prohibiting discrimination based on sexual orientation, it was not a good year for gay-rights advocates.

8. Taxes: Reform measures have been on the ballot since the initiative process was first established, but the movement gained strength after California's 1978 Proposition 13. In 2000, tax reform was a mixed bag. Tax cutters suffered some big defeats with voters in Alaska (property-tax relief), Colorado (lower taxes on certain items), and Oregon (full deduction of federal income taxes from state taxes). However, these losses were offset by big victories in Massachusetts (reducing income taxes), South Dakota (abolishing the inheritance tax), and Washington state (declaring null and void certain tax or fee increases adopted by state and local governments without voter approval).

9. Bilingual Education: Arizonans voted overwhelmingly to eliminate bilingual education. This strong showing, coupled with all the positive reports of the results of the 1997 passage of the first such initiative in California, makes it likely that initiatives like this will be on the ballots of other states in the near future.

10. Environmental Reform: This movement took a beating in 2000, with defeats in Arizona (growth limitations), Oregon ("takings" law), Colorado (growth limitations), Maine (clear cutting), and Missouri (banning of billboards). Its only major victory was in Florida, which passed an initiative creating a statewide rail system.

REGULATION OF THE INITIATIVE PROCESS

The initiative process has fallen prey to its own success. Lawmakers who have been most affected by this citizen's tool have struck back by imposing regulations on it. Often these regulations seem to serve no purpose other than to impede citizens use of the only means they have to influence unresponsive government. The initiative process may well be in need of review and reform, but state legislators seem to be acting in a vacuum, without taking time to understand the consequences of the regulations they impose. William Jennings Bryan said it best at the Nebraska Constitutional Convention in 1920:

We have the initiative and referendum; do not disturb them. If defects are discovered, correct them and perfect the machinery. . . . Make it possible for the people to have what they want. . . . We are the world's teacher in democracy; the world looks to us for an example. We cannot ask others to trust the people unless we are ourselves willing to trust them.

When the initiative process was established, many of the initiative states provided that these powers reserved to the people would be "self-executing." In other initiative states, the legislature was entrusted with creating procedures by which the people could exercise the initiative. Because of citizen concern about legislative efforts to limit initiative rights, in some states the legislature is instructed to enact laws designed only to facilitate, not to hinder, the initiative process. Nevertheless, in most of the states, the legislatures have enacted legislation that restricts rather than facilitates the use of these powers. These restrictions have often violated the citizens' First Amendment rights, as articulated by the U.S. Supreme Court in *Meyer v. Grant* (1998) and *Buckley v. American Constitutional Law Foundation* (1999).

Furthermore, the restrictions imposed on the citizenry are typically not imposed on others seeking to use a state's electoral process to bring about changes in state government, whether through lobbying, legislating, or running for political office. States do have a compelling interest in ensuring that all elections are conducted in a non-fraudulent manner. However, if legislatures wish to regulate lawmaking by the people, they should impose the same restrictions on others who are trying to influence government. For example, lobbyists who seek to have the legislature enact new laws or propose amendments to the state constitution typically are not subject to voter-registration or residency requirements, unlike those who collect signatures for initiatives. In the absence of evidence of voter fraud during this process, the purported purpose behind these legislatively imposed limitations on the citizenry should be viewed skeptically.

Some say that new regulations are needed because an unregulated initiative process represents "laws without government." But the initiative process in the United States is one of the most regulated in the world. The government tells you whether you can or cannot collect signatures on a certain issue, the number of subjects that can be included within the issue, the size of the petition you circulate, how many signatures you must collect and from what areas, what period of time you have to collect signatures, who can and cannot collect those signatures, and, ultimately, whether your issue can be on the ballot or not.

Another argument made for limiting the initiative process is that the people already have the ability to check government through elections; therefore the check available through initiatives is not necessary. However, most citizens use the process only to address single issues that their elected officials, for whatever reason, have not addressed. Voting officials out of office for failing to deal with one particular issue is an extreme step, far more extreme than allowing the people to make laws through occasional use of the initiative process. In a hundred years the people have made approximately eight hundred laws. That is not many, considering that an average state legislature passes more than a thousand laws a year.

Expansion of the initiative process is an uphill battle. Because citizens have been successful in passing reforms that have limited the power of government, legislators in states that do not have the initiative process have been wary of allowing it. This is, of course, a perfect illustration of why the process is needed.

After a hundred years of initiative use, we know that the citizens support it, not as a way to destroy representative democracy, but to ensure that they, the people, are the ultimate sovereigns, as the Founding Fathers intended. Representative government and the initiative process are perfect complements—two imperfect systems of governance, both designed to help the people, and both carefully constructed to balance the weaknesses of one with the strengths of the other.

CHAPTER EIGHT

Why Initiatives Are Necessary: Some Tales from California

Ron K. Unz

An initiative campaign in California in 1997 dismantled the system of so-called bilingual education—which really was Spanish-only instruction—for hundreds of thousands of students, possibly as many as a million, in California public schools. I was the main organizer of the initiative, and during the campaign I was often asked how I got involved in this issue. Part of the reason is that I come from somewhat of an immigrant background myself, in that my mother, though born in Los Angeles, grew up in a non-English-speaking household. Her parents were immigrants from Europe, and she learned their language at home. Then when she went to school she quickly and easily learned English. Because of her experience, bilingual education programs never made much sense to me. Why aren't young children taught English as soon as they start school? Why are they kept sometimes for years in programs where most of the instruction is in another language?

I first heard about bilingual education in the late seventies, and every few years the subject would make headlines again. There were stories about how unsuccessful these programs were, and how unpopular they were. Yet from just a small number of students in the 1970s bilin-

---

Ron K. Unz is the chairman of English for the Children and the chairman of Wall Street Analytics, a financial-services software firm that he founded in 1987. A theoretical physicist by training, he holds degrees from Harvard, Cambridge, and Stanford. He led the successful Proposition 227 campaign in California in 1997, which effectively eliminated nearly half of the country's programs of bilingual education.

gual education grew till in the mid-nineties close to three million immigrant students around the country were in native-language instruction. In February 1996 a series of articles in the *Los Angeles Times* described how a group of immigrant Latino parents in downtown Los Angeles actually had to start a public boycott of their local elementary school because it was refusing to teach their children English.

Things seemed to have reached the point of insanity. I started looking into the hard data on the California programs and found that the numbers were astonishing, much worse than I had imagined. Official government statistics coming from the state office of bilingual instruction showed that a quarter of all the children in California public schools—well over a million students—were classified as not knowing English. Of those students, only 5 or 6 per cent learned English every year. This meant that 95 per cent of the immigrant students who started a given school year classified as not knowing English were still classified as not knowing English by the end of that school year! That is extraordinary.

Furthermore, I found out that the law governing bilingual education in California had expired ten years before, and for ten straight years the state government had been deadlocked on whether to renew it. During that decade when legally the program no longer had a basis for existence, it had doubled in size. And a similar situation can be found in many other parts of the country today.

Seeking Successes

At that point I started considering the initiative process. A ballot initiative was really the only means of bringing change, since the state legislature had been deadlocked for ten years on doing something about a law that no longer existed. I thought that the first thing I should do was to talk with key supporters of bilingual education—individuals and academics and organizations—to get their side of the story. Although it looked on paper as if this program had a 95 per cent failure rate at teaching English, maybe I was missing something. And so I met with more than a dozen of the leading supporters of bilingual education across the country.

Early in the process I talked to the leaders of the National Council of La Raza, a Latino advocacy organization that is generally quite supportive of bilingual education. Since I had been very much on the pro-immigration side of the immigration wars that had taken place in California a few years earlier, I was on reasonably friendly terms with them. I said I was thinking of putting an initiative on the ballot in California to get rid of bilingual education because it doesn't work and asked them what they thought about the idea.

The first thing they all told me was that the system of bilingual education both in California and elsewhere in the United States was a tragedy. It was horrible that so many of these millions of immigrant children were having their education ruined by these disastrous programs. But they all went on to say that the problem was not in the *theory* of bilingual education but in the *practice*. The programs don't have enough teachers, they don't have the right teachers, they don't have enough money, they don't have enough institutional support; in their view, this accounted for the failure.

So then I asked them, "Can you point to any large-scale example anywhere in America in the last thirty years where a program like this has really worked?" They couldn't think of any. You could certainly find individual classrooms where it has worked, some individual schools where it seemed to be working, a few small school districts that seemed to have had some success; but nobody could point to a large-scale success. So then I said, "I'm a theoretical physicist by training, and in the sciences there's a big difference between theory and experiment. If your theory says something works but in experiment after experiment it has never worked, at some point you say, maybe the theory is wrong. Maybe it just doesn't work." Their only response was to point to researchers who had done studies claiming it really *did* work even though it didn't seem to work in practice.

Another thing I found out was that some of the theorists, especially the more academic ones, believe some strange things. Steve Kreshen is one of the leading lights in the academic firmament of bilingual education, and in a telephone conversation with him I said something like this: "Clearly, if we're talking about older children, children who came to the United States when they were twelve, thirteen, or fourteen and don't speak English, you can make a plausible case for teaching academic subjects in their native language while they're learning English so they don't fall behind academically. [I'm not saying I agree with that; most of the immigrant friends I talked with felt that even at that older age, it's much better for children to be taught in English immediately.] But the vast majority of the children we're talking about enter school when they're five or six. Over half of them are born in the United States. Since it's so quick and easy to learn another language at that age, why not teach them English as soon as they start school?" His answer was that this wasn't true, that research has conclusively shown that the *older* you are, the easier it is to learn another language! I had him repeat this a couple of times to make sure I had heard it correctly.

He and other bilingual theorists actually believe—and they claim they have evidence to prove it—that adults learn languages easier than teenagers, and teenagers learn languages easier than little children. That is part of the theoretical basis of the bilingual education programs that have been around for thirty years. They say it generally takes a young child five to seven years to learn another language. In fact, in the middle of the initiative campaign, some bilingual theorists at University of California–Riverside put out a new research report saying they had conclusively disproved the theory that it takes five to seven years for a child to learn English: it really takes *ten* years. In other words, a child who starts first grade not speaking English will probably have arrived at a pretty good knowledge of the language around the time he or she is a sophomore in high school!

Of course, most bilingual education programs include about half an hour of English and five and a half hours of the native language. A child whose entire family speaks Spanish at home, who watches Spanish TV and listens to Spanish radio, who lives in a neighborhood where everyone speaks Spanish, and who gets only thirty minutes of English in school—maybe it does take ten years for that child to learn English.

In the years just preceding our campaign, California had been through some very divisive, ethnically charged initiatives dealing with such issues as immigration, illegal immigration, and affirmative action. I felt it was very important for this measure not to come across as politically partisan and certainly not to seem in any way anti-Latino or anti-immigrant. Early on I met with a lot of the key Latino political leaders in the state, and some of the meetings were really fascinating. Privately, many of these leaders were very encouraging. This ran contrary to the prediction of a lot of my conservative friends. "We hate bilingual education," they said, "but boy, those Latino Democrats love it. They'll fight you tooth and nail. And the teacher unions really love bilingual education. They're going to be your biggest foes." To some extent that is true. But on the other hand, Albert Shanker, the founder of the American Federation of Teachers—the founder, really, of the modern teacher-union movement—was also the most vehement critic of bilingual education in the United States for about twenty years. And right around the time I filed the initiative I met with one of the most senior teacher-union leaders in California. He basically said: "The emperor has no clothes. Bilingual education has never worked. We've been trying to do something about it for some twenty years, with no luck at all."

The Power of the Few

In the dynamics of modern legislative politics, a very small group of people can block change if they feel very strongly about it, even if the vast majority of people are on the other side. The group that kept bilingual education in place in California for twenty or thirty years was the California Association of Bilingual Educators—5,000 members, many of whom are not even active members, in a state population of 35 million. On a number of occasions the big teacher unions and other educational powers had tried, not to eliminate bilingual education, but to modify it, reform it, or put a cap on it. Their efforts were always blocked by a 5,000-member trade association, which supported it partly for ideological reasons, partly because members each received a $5,000 annual bonus for being a bilingual education teacher, and partly, I think, because if they admitted that it didn't work, they would have to recognize that their efforts had adversely affected the lives of thousands upon thousands of immigrant children over the last twenty years. That would be a very difficult thing to admit.

Most of these people are very sincere and well-intentioned. Bilingual education was established in the late sixties and early seventies with the best of motives: to help immigrant children. Unfortunately, by the time people found out it wasn't working very well, an industry—teachers, administrators, textbook manufacturers, academic theorists—was in place, and that industry has fought very effectively to maintain and expand itself. The people behind bilingual education were not the union activists, not the Latino politicians, not Latino immigrants, not the rest of society—those groups for the most part hated bilingual education—but a small number of ethnic activists who had originally created these programs and the bilingual-education industry.

During and after the campaign the polls showed that the views of ordinary people on this issue are very clear cut. The question that most of the newspaper polls in California asked during the campaign was neutrally phrased: "There is a proposal to require all public school instruction to be conducted in English, and for children not fluent in English to be placed in a one-year intensive English immersion program.

Do you support it or do you oppose it?" The polls in California tended to show between 70 and 80 per cent support. Around the rest of the country the support is very similar. After the campaign I did some huge national polls—which aren't all that expensive if you do them the right way, through reputable polling organizations—and they found between 77 and 98 per cent support nationwide. In New York state a separate poll showed 79 per cent support. This support cuts across boundaries: Anglos and Latinos, blacks and whites, Jews, born-again Christians, union members, liberals and conservatives—in all these groups we found support of nearly 80 per cent.

The campaign ended up being just what I'd hoped—one of the most bipartisan campaigns in California political history: it was opposed by both political parties. We were opposed by the chairman of the state Republican party and the chairman of the state Democratic party, by all four candidates for governor, and by President Bill Clinton. We were opposed by nearly all the state newspapers, nearly all the unions, all the educational organizations. Now, some of these groups, when I met with them privately, seemed to have very mixed feelings about the whole thing. But they lined up to defend the status quo. There wasn't any organized anti-bilingual group that had been around for twenty years giving political contributions and going to candidate forums. In fact, at all the public forums I participated in—and I probably did fifty or sixty public debates during that campaign, as well as a lot of electronic debates—anybody who tried to estimate what support there was in California for this measure would probably have guessed between 1 and 2 per cent.

Usually these forums seemed to be unanimously on the other side. If there were two hundred people in the audience, you could safely assume nearly all of them were against the initiative. Sometimes one or two were neutral, and occasionally we could actually get one supporter. The only people who come to public forums on the issue of bilingual education are bilingual-education teachers and administrators. They're the people who put pressure on the politicians by speaking out. But when I did radio debates, whether the radio station was liberal or conservative, nearly all the callers were supportive of the initiative. People would say, "I'm left of left, but I really support this measure"—because, again, teaching children English is something very commonsensical. Even though this is described as a highly controversial issue, in many ways it was probably the most non-controversial measure you could imagine.

Suppose we could go back to the 1950s, a time when there was a sharp ideological divide in the United States—left versus right, Communist versus anti-Communist. There were lots of fierce debates. Suppose we went around to members of those different debating groups and said, "There's a proposal to require that all immigrant children be taught English when they go to school. Do you support it or oppose it?" I think most of them would have said, "Of course we support it. What alternative could there possibly be?" You probably would have gotten 80 to 90 per cent support on that issue in the 1950s, and amazingly enough, today you still get 80 per cent support. But interest-group politics behind closed doors can exert disproportionate weight.

To win this campaign, all we really had to do was to put the measure on the ballot. We spent very little money on advertising; the other side spent twenty-five times as much on advertising as we did. They had a big budget, an organized campaign staff, and a top political consultant. They had a very good commercial in which all four candidates for governor said, "Vote no on the initiative"; it was named the best spot of the year in a losing campaign. And we still ended up winning by the largest landslide any contested initiative had had in twenty years in California.

Why the Initiative Is Needed

If a measure is put on the ballot, the silent majority can then speak through their vote. That is one reason why I am in favor of the initiative process, even though it can be misused. It certainly can be taken too far. In fact, I am quite opposed to anything like a *federal* initiative process. I also do not think we should make it much easier to place initiatives on the ballot, because then there would be too many introduced in order to satisfy people's personal whims or egos. But having the initiative process available as a safety valve for things that almost everybody believes in but that have simply been stymied by small interest-group politics— 5,000 people in a state of 35 million blocking change for twenty or thirty years—is what makes it really necessary.

Furthermore, that process can do a lot to inform the public. One of the collateral benefits of our campaign in California is that we focused more media attention on bilingual education in that one-year period than had been given to the issue during the preceding thirty years. There were numerous in-depth investigative reports across the political spectrum, and they all came essentially to the same conclusion. In fact, even though opposition to bilingual education is regarded as a conservative cause, what I consider the single best account of the initiative campaign appeared in *The Nation*, a left liberal publication. The initiative process and the media attention sparked a debate that I think is having a very positive impact in other states and possibly at the federal level as well.

Another sign of the need for the initiative is that in the two years since it passed in California—overwhelmingly popular, overwhelmingly successful—I have been unable to get any political leader of any stature in either political party to do so much as endorse it. I've shown them polling numbers. In some cases I've even shown them with polling data that their support for this measure would cause a massive swing in their direction when they're running in a difficult race. They're all scared of the issue. They say it's too controversial, too difficult to deal with. And so, if it were not for the initiative process in other states, I think the California solution would probably not be replicated elsewhere. If a few more state initiatives win, and if the impressive rise in the test scores of a million immigrant students in California—as reported in a front-page *New York Times* story in August 2000—continues, then maybe at some point Congress will do something about bilingual education. But I'm not holding my breath.

That is why direct democracy through ballot initiatives really does have a place in the political process.

Notes

Chapter One: THE FOUNDERS' VIEWS
Charles R. Kesler

1. In the best contemporaneous study of the subject, published in 1900, Ellis Paxson Oberholtzer admits that the terms "initiative" and "referendum" were unknown to "otherwise intelligent and well informed men" until very recently. "As for myself," he writes, "I cannot remember that very much that was definite was known of this interesting democratic institution prior to the appearance of a popularly written work on the Swiss Confederation in 1889. . . . This book started discussion in this country, and it soon came to be recognized that law-making by the people was also no strange thing in the United States." See Ellis Paxson Oberholtzer, *The Referendum in America* (New York: Scribner's, 1900), v. Another important early study was the chapter on "Direct Legislation by the People" in James Bryce, *The American Commonwealth* (New York: Macmillan, 1893), 1:463–476. Whole books were written to prove that the referendum was not a recent Swiss export but a venerable American tradition, or at least an American contribution to a much older tradition. Cf. Charles Sumner Lobingier, *The People's Law, or Popular Participation in Law-Making, from Ancient Folk-Moot to Modern Referendum* (New York: Macmillan, 1909).

2. Cf. Woodrow Wilson, "The Study of Administration," *Political Science Quarterly* 2 (June 1887): 204–9.

3. Lobingier, *The People's Law*, 1–77, 100, 338.

4. Ibid., iii, 124–25.

5. Lewis Jerome Johnson, "Direct Legislation as an Ally of Representative Government," in William Bennett Munro, ed., *The Initiative, Referendum, and Recall* (New York: Appleton, 1912), 152, 161–62.

6. For a good summary of the functions of town meetings, see Lobingier, *The People's Law*, 99–102.

7. Albert Lawrence Lowell, "The Referendum in the United States," in Munro, *The Initiative, Referendum, and Recall*, 127; Lobingier, *The People's Law*, 164–67, 169–79, 182–83, 189–90; Oberholtzer, *The Referendum in America*, 103–7.

8. Lobingier, *The People's Law*, 167–68, 180–81.

9. Ibid., 102–4; Oberholtzer, *The Referendum in America*, 110–11.

10. Consider Clinton Rossiter, ed., *The Federalist Papers*, with a new introduction and notes by Charles R. Kesler (New York: Penguin Putnam, 1999), No. 9, 41–42.

11. Lowell, "The Referendum in the United States," 127; Lobingier, *The*

People's Law, 338–39. Cf. Oberholtzer, *The Referendum in America*, 100: "It appears to have occurred to no one of all our leading democrats of the Revolutionary period, not even Franklin or Paine or any of the rest of the ostentatious friends of the people in Pennsylvania, that a constitution to be valid needs be submitted to popular vote." Still, in Pennsylvania, military operations during the Revolution prevented a planned recurrence to the people for their opinion on replacing the existing constitution. Rhode Island, too, is a mixed case, where the proposed federal Constitution of 1787 was referred to town meetings, where it was rejected, only to have the state assembly eventually authorize a ratification convention, with delegates chosen by the towns, which finally approved the document in 1790. See Oberholtzer, *The Referendum in America*, 17–27, 48–51, 60–65, 101–3; and Lobingier, *The People's Law*, 190–94.

12. John Adams, *A Defence of the Constitutions of Government of the United States*, in Charles Francis Adams, ed., *The Works of John Adams* (Boston: Little, Brown, 1850–56), 6:6–7.

13. In 1777, Alexander Hamilton contrasted "representative democracy" with the "error, confusion, and instability" of direct democracy in a remarkable letter to Gouverneur Morris, cited in Gordon S. Wood, *The Creation of the American Republic, 1776–1787* (Chapel Hill: University of North Carolina Press, 1969), 224–25. John Adams used the term "representative democracy," though in a somewhat different sense, in 1787 in his *Defence of the Constitutions of Government*, in Adams, *Works*, 5:454.

14. Aristotle, *Politics*, 1278b5–1279b10.

15. Aristotle, *Politics*, 1279b11–1281a39; Plato, *Republic*, 422e–423a, 551d.

16. Aristotle, *Politics*, 1281a39–1284b34, 1295a25–1297a13; Cicero, *De Re Publica*, I.45, 69.

17. See Harvey C. Mansfield, Jr., "Modern and Medieval Representation," in J. R. Pennock and J. Chapman, eds., *Nomos 11: Representation* (New York: Atherton Press, 1968), 55–82, at 77–80. Willi Paul Adams points out that "republican" was a "smear word" in America until 1776, when Thomas Paine in *Common Sense* launched both an all-out attack on the British Constitution and a full-throated defense of republicanism. After that, "republic" and "democracy" tended to be used interchangeably in the United States until the debate over the Constitution. Willi Paul Adams, *The First American Constitutions: Republican Ideology and the Making of the State Constitutions in the Revolutionary Era*, trans. Rita and Robert Kimber (Chapel Hill: University of North Carolina Press, 1980), 99–117.

18. Rossiter, *The Federalist Papers*, No. 9, 40. Cf. No. 14, 68–69, and No. 63, 354–55.

19. For an explanation of the remarkable change implied here in the political bearing of Christianity, see Harry V. Jaffa, *A New Birth of Freedom: Abraham Lincoln and the Coming of the Civil War* (Lanham, Md.: Rowman & Littlefield, 2000), chap. 2.

20. James Otis, "The Rights of the British Colonies Asserted and Proved," in Bernard Bailyn, ed., *Pamphlets of the American Revolution, 1750–1776* (Cam-

bridge: Harvard University Press, 1965), 408–82, at 445–46.

21. Daniel Dulany, "Considerations on the Propriety of Imposing Taxes in the British Colonies for the Purpose of Raising a Revenue," in Bailyn, *Pamphlets*, 598–658, at 610–21.

22. Hanna Fenichel Pitkin, *The Concept of Representation* (Berkeley: University of California Press, 1967), 144–67; cf. 191–98.

23. See *The Writings and Speeches of Edmund Burke* (Boston: Little, Brown, 1901), 2:95–96.

24. See Herbert J. Storing, ed., *The Complete Anti-Federalist* (Chicago: University of Chicago Press, 1981), 2:230 (2.8.15).

25. Ibid., 379 (2.9.42).

26. *The Essex Result*, in Charles S. Hyneman and Donald S. Lutz, eds., *American Political Writing during the Founding Era, 1760–1805* (Indianapolis: Liberty Press, 1983), 1:480–522, at 496.

27. See Terence Ball, "'A Republic—If You Can Keep It,'" in Terence Ball and J. G. A. Pocock, eds., *Conceptual Change and the Constitution* (Lawrence: University Press of Kansas, 1988), 137–164, at 145–48.

28. Thus Brutus begins by extolling the "different classes" and "several orders" of society, e.g., "the farmer, merchant, mecanick, and other various orders of people" but soon finds himself warning that "the great body of the yeomen" will be sacrificed to "the natural aristocracy" or "the rich," and eventually concludes that the proposed Constitution "will literally be a government in the hands of the few to oppress and plunder the many." In Storing, *The Complete Anti-Federalist*, 2:380–81 (2.9.42).

29. Storing, *The Complete Anti-Federalist*, 2:368-69 (2.9.11–2.9.15). In his 1782 election sermon, Zabdiel Adams commented on the second-best status of representation. "Government by deputation does not consist with that plenitude of liberty in the people that they might enjoy, could they give their suffrages personally. However, when our representatives are regularly chosen, are amenable to our tribunals, and their election is not of long duration, then we may be said to be as free as the state of the world will commonly admit." Hyneman and Lutz, *American Political Writing*, 1:539–564, at 543–544. On democracy's employment of lot and election, see Montesquieu, *The Spirit of the Laws*, Book II, chap. 2; and Bernard Manin, *The Principles of Representative Government* (Cambridge: Cambridge University Press, 1997), chaps. 1–2.

30. Russell L. Hanson describes the Anti-Federalists' opinion as follows: "Just because rulers were likely to become corrupt, direct democracy was the preferred arrangement, but this was acknowledged to be impractical in a society of any great extent." "'Commons' and 'Commonwealth' at the American Founding: Democratic Republicanism as the New American Hybrid," in Ball and Pocock, *Conceptual Change*, 165–93, at 191 n. 34.

31. John Phillip Reid, *The Concept of Representation in the Age of the American Revolution* (Chicago: University of Chicago Press, 1989), 98–99.

32. See *Annals of Congress: The Debates and Proceedings in the Congress of

the United States, 42 vol. (Washington, D.C.: Gales & Seaton, 1834-56), 1:733–45.

33. Consider the instructions of the townsmen of Pittsfield, Massachusetts, to their representatives at the state constitutional convention, which conclude: "On the whole, we empower you to act agreeable to the dictates of your own judgment after you have heard all the reasonings upon the various subjects of disquisition, having an invariable respect to the true liberty and real happiness of this State throughout all generations, any instructions herein contained to the contrary notwithstanding." In Robert J. Taylor, ed., *Massachusetts, Colony to Commonwealth: Documents on the Formation of Its Constitution, 1775–1780* (Chapel Hill: University of North Carolina Press, 1961), 117–19, at 119.

34. Rossiter, *The Federalist Papers*, No. 37, 195; No. 51, 290; No. 63, 351.

35. Noah Webster, "An Oration on the Anniversary of the Declaration of Independence" (1802), in Hyneman and Lutz, *American Political Writing*, 2:1220–40, at 1231–32.

36. Rossiter, *The Federalist Papers*, No. 10, 49. "Without mentioning Montesquieu by name," Terence Ball notes, "Madison rejects the heretofore unchallenged Montesquieuan idea that a republic can be a democracy." Ball, "'A Republic—If You Can Keep It,'" 143. See Montesquieu, *The Spirit of the Laws*, Book II, chap. 2. The Montesquieuan typology was well known. Cf. the Anti-Federalist writer "Agrippa," who explained, "Republicks are divided into democraticks, and aristocraticks." In Storing, *The Complete Anti-Federalist*, 4:103 (4.6.60).

37. Rossiter, *The Federalist Papers*, No. 10, 50.

38. The large size of the electoral districts in the large republic will also discourage corruption in gaining and holding office, according to Madison. Ibid., No. 10, 50.

39. Ibid., No. 63, 355, emphasis in the original. Cf. Montesquieu, *The Spirit of the Laws*, Book II, chap. 2.

40. Cf. James Wilson, who in the Pennsylvania ratifying convention on Dec. 4, 1787, declared that in the Constitution "*all authority, of every kind, is derived by* REPRESENTATION *from the* PEOPLE, *and the* DEMOCRATIC PRINCIPLE *is carried into every part of government.*" Cited in Hanson, "'Commons' and 'Commonwealth,'" 182 and 192 n. 54. Obviously, not all supporters of the Constitution adhered to Madison's sharp distinction between democracy and republican government. In fact, Madison himself, having made the distinction in *Federalist* No. 10 and having thereby discredited "pure democracy," uses the terms more loosely in later *Federalist* essays. The real distinction "between the American and other republics" is not so much the presence or absence of representation, he confesses in No. 63, but that in America the principle achieves "its full effect," namely, "the total exclusion" of the people in their collective capacity from any share in administering their government. Here these "other republics" include "the most pure democracies of Greece." Rossiter, *The Federalist*, No. 63, 354–55.

41. Rossiter, *The Federalist Papers*, No. 49, 283, 285; No. 63, 352; No. 71, 400; No. 78, 435.

42. Ibid., No. 49, 283–85; No. 78, 435.

Chapter Three: LINCOLN'S VIEW OF DIRECT DEMOCRACY
Herman Belz

1. Roy P. Basler et al., eds., *The Collected Works of Abraham Lincoln*, 9 vols. (New Brunswick, N.J.: Rutgers University Press, 1953-55), 3:94. (Hereafter cited as *Collected Works*.) This edition is available on the Web in searchable form at www.hti.umich.edu/l/lincoln.

2. Yves R. Simon, *Philosophy of Democratic Government* (Chicago: University of Chicago Press, 1951), 144–54. Simon refers to this idea as the "coach driver" theory of democracy. He observes that although not decisive in the early American democracy, it was an ideological factor of some importance in American history from the time of Andrew Jackson (p. 149).

3. Slavko Splichal, *Public Opinion: Developments and Controversies in the Twentieth Century* (Lanham, Md.: Rowman & Littlefield, 1999), ix, 1–7, 20–24.

4. Splichal associates Lincoln's position on public opinion with that of Edmund Burke, who held to the "independent" rather than "mandate" theory of the relationship between a representative and public opinion. Indicating Lincoln's significance in the history of public opinion, Splichal writes: "Different meanings of publicness that were formed from the Renaissance on were summed up in the famous statement uttered by Abraham Lincoln during the U.S. Civil War, in which he paraphrased the conception of the people's governance first outlined by Edmund Burke: 'government of the people [with their consent], by the people [through their representatives], for the people [for their common and permanent good] shall not perish from the earth.'" Splichal, *Public Opinion*, 17.

5. Michael Schudson, *The Good Citizen: A History of American Civil Life* (Cambridge: Harvard University Press, 1998), 90–132.

6. *Collected Works*, 3:363.

7. Ibid., 8:394.

8. Simon, *Philosophy of Democratic Government*, 187; Bertrand de Jouvenel, *On Power: The Natural History of Its Growth* (Indianapolis: Liberty Fund, 1993), 274.

9. *Collected Works*, 1:108–9, 111–12.

10. Ibid., 1:278.

11. Michael Zuckert, "Lincoln and the Problem of Civil Religion," 18-25, MS, in possession of the author. Lincoln affirmed the right of revolution in a speech on the Mexican War in 1848. Referring to the revolution by which Texas became an independent republic, he said: "Any people anywhere, being inclined, and having the power, have the right to rise up, and shake off the existing government, and form a new one that suits them better. This is a most valuable,—a most sacred right—a right, which we hope and believe, is to liberate the world." *Collected Works*, 1:438–39.

12. Ibid., 1:348.

13. Ibid., 2:243.

14. Ibid., 3:247, 273.

15. Ibid., 2:267.

16. Ibid., 2:269–70.

17. Ibid., 2:321–22.

18. Ibid., 3:385.

19. Ibid., 2:514; 3:18, 27.

20. Ibid., 2:266.

21. Ibid., 3:315–16.

22. Ibid., 3:316.

23. Ibid., 2:322.

24. Jesse T. Carpenter, *The South as a Conscious Minority 1789–1861: A Study in Political Thought* (New York, 1930; reprint 1963), 200–213. Yves Simon states that in direct democracy each member of society possesses a personal right of consent to law, legal obligation depending on personal volition. He observes that to apply this theory with strict consistency would be to destroy society by secession. *Philosophy of Democratic Government*, 150–54.

25. *Congressional Globe*, 36th Cong., 2d Sess., 11 February 1861, 853.

26. Jeffrey K. Tulis, *The Rhetorical Presidency* (Princeton, N.J.: Princeton University Press, 1987), 4–5, 79–83.

27. *Collected Works*, 4:200, 175.

28. Ibid., 4:207.

29. Ibid., 4:264–65.

30. Ibid., 4:267, 269.

31. Ibid., 4:265.

32. Thomas J. Pressly, "Ballots and Bullets: Lincoln and the Right of Revolution," *American Historical Review* 67 (1962): 660.

33. *Collected Works*, 4:268.

34. Ibid., 4:270.

35. Harry V. Jaffa, *A New Birth of Freedom: Abraham Lincoln and the Coming of the Civil War* (Lanham, Md.: Rowman & Littlefield, 2000), 191.

36. *Collected Works*, 4:332.

37. Ibid., 4:428.

38. Ibid., 6:27–28.

Chapter Four: BEYOND REFERENDUM DEMOCRACY
James S. Fishkin

1. For more on plebiscitary democracy and its contrast with deliberative institutions, see my *Democracy and Deliberation: New Directions for Democratic Reform* (New Haven and London: Yale University Press, 1991).

2. George Gallup, "Public Opinion in a Democracy" (Princeton: The Stafford Little Lectures, 1938).

3. The term comes from Anthony Downs, *An Economic Theory of Democracy* (New York: Harper and Row: 1957). For a good overview of the current

state of research on the limited knowledge of the American mass public, see Michael Delli Carpini and Scott Keeter, *What Americans Know About Politics and Why It Matters* (New Haven: Yale University Press, 1996).

4. James Madison, *Notes of Debates in the Federal Convention of 1787 Reported by James Madison*, with an introduction by Adrienne Koch (New York: Norton, 1987), 40.

5. Jack N. Rakove, *Original Meanings: Politics and Ideas in the Making of the Constitution* (New York: Vintage Books, 1997), 203.

6. Herbert Storing, ed., *The Complete Anti-Federalist* (Chicago: University of Chicago Press, 1981), 2:265.

7. "Rhode Island's Assembly Refuses to Call a Convention and Submits the Constitution Directly to the People," in Bernard Bailyn, ed., *The Debate on the Constitution,* Part 2 (New York: Library of America, 1993), 271.

8. "The Freemen of Providence Submit Eight Reasons for Calling a Convention," in Bailyn, *The Debate*, 280.

9. See Edmund S. Morgan, "Safety in Numbers: Madison, Hume and the Tenth Federalist," *Huntington Library Quarterly* (1986): 95-112; see 105. Even this premise seems to assume that the politicians will be offering rather than receiving the bribes or inducements. No one in Madison's time could have envisaged television and the enormous appetites for campaign funding that it creates, rendering politicians who wish to be re-elected in need of so much financial support that the collection of campaign money comes perilously close to bribery, offered by factions and interests.

10. For a classic statement of the dilemma, see Hanna Pitkin, *The Concept of Representation* (Berkeley: University of California Press, 1967), chap. 7. Pitkin does not consider the middle-ground position sketched here and is (in my view) unduly dismissive of the Madisonian "filter" (pp. 194-95).

11. Testimony of Samuel H. Beer before the House Judiciary Committee, Dec. 8, 1998; emphasis added.

12. See, for example, Representative Lindsey Graham discussing the public's views on impeachment: "They have an impression about this case from just tons . . . of talk, tons . . . of spin. . . . The question you must ask: If every American were required to do what I have done, which is sit silently and listen to the evidence, would it be different?" CNN transcript, Jan. 16, 1999.

13. Samuel Popkin, *The Reasoning Voter* (University of Chicago Press, 1991), and Arthur Lupia, "Shortcuts Versus Encyclopedias: Information and Voting Behavior in California Insurance Reform Elections," *American Political Science Review* 88 (1994): 63-76.

14. Robert Luskin "From Denial to Extenuation (and Finally Beyond): Political Sophistication and Citizen Performance," in J. Kuklinski, ed., *Thinking about Political Psychology* (New York: Cambridge University Press, forthcoming).

15. For more on how this works, see James Fishkin and Robert Luskin, "Bringing Deliberation to the Democratic Dialogue," in Max M. McCombs, ed., *A Poll with a Human Face: The National Issues Convention Experiment in Political*

Communication (Mahwah: N.J.: Lawrence Elbaum, 1999), and James S. Fishkin, *The Voice of the People: Public Opinion and Democracy*, expanded ed. (New Haven and London: Yale University Press, 1997).

16. For more information, see www.i-d-a.com.au, the website of Issues Deliberation Australia, whose managing director, Dr. Pam Ryan, provided the leadership that created the Australian Deliberative Poll. I would also like to thank colleagues John Higley, Robert Luskin, and Ian McAllister for their work on this collaborative effort.

Chapter Five: POLLING AND THE VIRTUAL PUBLIC
Benjamin Ginsberg

1. See Steven J. Rosenstone and John Mark Hansen, *Mobilization, Participation and Democracy in America* (New York: Macmillan, 1993).

2. Matthew Crenson and Benjamin Ginsberg, "Party Politics and Personal Democracy," in *American Political Parties: Decline or Resurgence?* (Washington, D.C.: Congressional Quarterly Press, 2001).

3. Al Gore, *Creating Government that Works Better and Costs Less,* Report of the National Performance Review (U.S. Government Printing Office, 1993).

4. Richard Jensen, *The Winning of the Midwest* (Chicago: University of Chicago Press, 1971), chap. 6.

5. See Mark Wahlgren Summers, *The Press Gang: Newspapers and Politics, 1863–1878* (Chapel Hill: University of North Carolina Press, 1994).

6. The classical description of nineteenth-century American political parties in action is Moisei Ostrogorski, *Democracy and the Organization of Political Parties* (New York: Macmillan, 1902).

7. See Angus Campbell, "Change in the American Electorate," in Angus Campbell and Philip E. Converse, eds., *The Human Meaning of Social Change* (New York: Russell Sage Foundation, 1972), 263–337.

8. J. Morgan Kousser, *The Shaping of Southern Politics: Suffrage Restriction and the Establishment of the One-Party South, 1890–1910* (New Haven: Yale University Press, 1974).

9. U.S. Bureau of the Census, *Statistical Abstract of the United States* (Washington, D.C., 1998). The most current data are regularly posted on the Census Bureau's website: www.census.gov/population/socdemo/voting/history/vot23.txt.

10. Melissa Feld, "Campaign Spending in 1996," MA thesis, Johns Hopkins University, 1999.

11. Steven E. Schier, *By Invitation Only: Contemporary Party, Interest Group and Campaign Strategies* (Pittsburgh: University of Pittsburgh Press, 2000).

12. Dana Milbank, "Virtual Politics: Candidates' Consultants Create the Customized Campaign," *The New Republic*, July 5, 1999, 22–27.

13. See, e.g., David Broder, "GOP to Spend $100 Million to Boost Turnout: Effort Will Target Wavering Voters and Weak Partisans," *Washington Post*, August 7, 2000, A1.

14. See Robert Shogan, "Politicians Embrace Status Quo as Nonvoter Numbers Grow," *Los Angeles Times*, May 4, 1998, A5. Also, Lars-Erik Nelson, "Undemocratic Vistas," *New York Review of Books*, August 12, 1999, 9–12.

15. Stephen Ansolabehere and Shanto Iyengar, *Going Negative: How Political Advertisements Shrink and Polarize the Electorate* (New York: Free Press, 1995).

16. Elizabeth Drew, *The Corruption of American Politics: What Went Wrong and Why* (New York: Birch Lane, 1999). Also, E. J. Dionne, Jr., *Why Americans Hate Politics* (New York: Simon and Schuster, 1991). See also Joseph S. Nye, Philip D. Zelikow, and David C. King, eds., *Why People Don't Trust Government* (Cambridge: Harvard University Press, 1997).

17. See David Canon, "A Pox on Both Your Parties," in David T. Canon, Anne M Khademian, and Kenneth R. Mayer, eds., *The Enduring Debate* (New York: Norton, 2000), 3.

18. E. E. Schattschneider, *The Semi-Sovereign People* (New York: Holt, 1960), chap. 4.

19. Shogan, "Politicians Embrace Status Quo."

20. Ibid.

21. Joan Didion, "Uncovered Washington," *New York Review of Books,"* June 24, 1999, 72–80.

22. See Ruy Teixeira and Joel Rogers, *America's Forgotten Majority: Why the White Working Class Still Matters* (New York: Basic Books, 2000). Also, Milton J. Esman, *Government Works: Why Americans Need the Feds* (Ithaca, N.Y.: Cornell University Press, 2000).

23. Christopher Lasch, *The Revolt of the Elites* (New York: Norton, 1995).

24. Helen Dewar, "Motor Voter Agreement Is Reached," *Washington Post*, April 28, 1993, A6.

25. Peter Baker, "Motor Voter Apparently Didn't Drive Up Turnout," *Washington Post*, November 6, 1996, B7.

26. George Gallup and Saul Rae, *The Pulse of Democracy: The Public Opinion Poll and How it Works* (New York: Simon and Schuster, 1940), 14. See also Charles W. Roll and Albert H. Cantril, *Polls: Their Use and Misuse in Politics* (Cabin John, Md.: Seven Locks Press, 1972).

27. See Benjamin Ginsberg, *The Captive Public* (New York: Basic Books, 1986). Also, Susan Herbst, *Numbered Voices* (Chicago: University of Chicago Press, 1993). See also J. D. Peters, "Historical Tensions in the Concept of Public Opinion," in T. L. Glasser and C. T. Salmon, eds., *Public Opinion and the Communication of Consent* (New York: Guilford Press, 1995), 3–32.

28. Chester F. Bernard, "Public Opinion in a Democracy" (Herbert Baker Foundation, Princeton University, 1939, pamphlet), 13.

29. Of course, not all polls claim scientific objectivity. The non-binding Iowa Republican presidential "straw poll," for example, does not use a random sample of Iowans. This poll counts only the votes of those Iowa Republicans who make the effort to travel to Iowa State University in Ames to indicate

which aspirants for the Republican presidential nomination they prefer. Political professionals and the media see the Iowa straw poll as an early indication of each candidate's strength. However, in its twenty-year history the straw poll has never predicted the eventual presidential winner. See Richard L. Berke, "Iowa Straw Poll Proving a Little Can Mean a Lot," *New York Times*, August 13, 1999, A1.

30. See Eugene Webb et al., *Unobtrusive Measures: Nonreactive Research in the Social Sciences* (Chicago: Rand McNally, 1966).

31. This discussion is based upon Ginsberg, *The Captive Public*.

32. For an excellent review of the actual process of opinion polling see Michael Traugott and Paul Lavrakas, *The Voter's Guide to Election Polls* (Chatham, N.J.: Chatham House, 1996).

33. Hadley Cantril, "The Intensity of an Attitude," *Journal of Abnormal and Social Psychology* 41 (1946): 129–35.

34. For the classic study see Aage R. Clausen, Philip Converse, and Warren Miller, "Electoral Myth and Reality: The 1964 Election," *American Political Science Review* 59 (June 1965): 321–32.

35. Dan Balz, "Rallying the Faithful for Gore: As Candidate Takes the Reins, Speakers Aim at Core Voters," *Washington Post*, August 16, 2000, A1.

36. Charles W. Roll, Jr., and Hadley Cantril, *Polls* (New York: Basic Books, 1972), 153.

37. See Richard Jensen, "American Election Analysis," in Seymour Martin Lipset, ed., *Politics and the Social Sciences* (New York: Oxford University Press, 1969), 229.

38. Rich Morin, "Telling Polls Apart," *Washington Post*, August 16, 2000, A35.

39. Fritz Morstein Marx, *The Administrative State* (Chicago: University of Chicago Press, 1957), 44.

40. Steven Cohen and William Eimicke, *The New Effective Public Manager* (San Francisco: Josey-Bass, 1995), chap.10.

41. The phrase "reinvention of government" is usually attributed to David Osborne and Ted Gaebler, *Reinventing Government* (Reading, Mass.: Addison-Wesley, 1992). The NPR report is published as *Creating a Government That Works Better and Costs Less*, Report of the National Performance Review (U.S. Government Printing Office, 1993).

42. Peri E. Arnold, *Making the Managerial Presidency: Comprehensive Reorganization Planning, 1905-1980* (Princeton: Princeton University Press, 1986).

43. Hoover Commission Report (New York: McGraw Hill, 1949), 3. See also Ronald C. Moe, *The Hoover Commissions Revisited* (Boulder, Colo.: Westview, 1982).

44. James Q. Wilson, "Reinventing Public Administration," *PS: Political Science and Politics*, December 1994.

45. NPR, *Creating a Government That Works Better*, 30.

46. Gerald Garvey, "The NPR in Historical Perspective," in Donald Kettl and John J. DiIulio, eds., *Inside the Reinvention Machine: Appraising Governmental Reform* (Washington, D.C.: Brookings, 1995), 104.

Chapter Six: FOR THE PEOPLE
G. Alan Tarr

1. These figures are compiled from data provided by the website of the Initiative and Referendum Institute: www.iandrinstitute.org

2. Illustrative scholarly critiques of direct democracy include David G. Lawrence, *California: The Politics of Diversity* (Minneapolis: West Publishing, 1995); Hans A. Linde, "When Initiative Lawmaking Is Not Republican Government: The Campaign Against Homosexuality," *Oregon Law Review* 72 (1993): 20–39; and Linda Fountain, "Lousy Lawmaking: Questioning the Desirability and Constitutionality of Legislating by Initiative," *Southern California Law Review* 61 (1998): 733–76. For a journalistic broadside against direct democracy, see David S. Broder, *Democracy Derailed: Initiative Campaigns and the Power of Money* (New York: Harcourt, 2000).

3. Joseph M. Bessette, *The Mild Voice of Reason: Deliberative Democracy and American National Government* (Chicago: University of Chicago Press, 1994).

4. All quotations are from Alexander Hamilton, James Madison, and John Jay, *The Federalist Papers*, ed. Clinton Rossiter (New York: New American Library, 1961): No. 63 at 384; No. 10 at 82; No. 71 at 432; No. 10 at 82; and No. 10 at 77.

5. This position is developed in greater detail in G. Alan Tarr, *Understanding State Constitutions* (Princeton, N.J.:Princeton University Press, 1998).

6. See, also, for example, North Carolina Constitution of 1776, art. 1; Massachusetts Constitution of 1780, preamble; and New Hampshire Constitution of 1784, Bill of Rights, art. 1. For discussion of these provisions, see Donald S. Lutz, *Popular Consent and Popular Control: Whig Political Theory in the Early State Constitutions* (Baton Rouge: Louisiana State University Press, 1980), chaps. 2–3; Akhil Reed Amar, "The Consent of the Governed," *Columbia Law Review* 94 (March 1994); and Christian G. Fritz, "Alternative Visions of American Constitutionalism: Popular Sovereignty and the Early American Constitutional Debate," *Hastings Constitutional Law Quarterly* 24 (Winter 1997): 287–357.

7. Alexis de Tocqueville, *Democracy in America*, ed. J. P. Mayer (New York: Harper & Row, 1966), 273.

8. *The Writings of Thomas Jefferson* (Washington, 1907), 7:423 (14 July 1789).

9. These differences are discussed in Shannon C. Stimson, *The American Revolution in Law; Anglo-American Jurisprudence before John Marshall* (Princeton, N.J.: Princeton University Press, 1990).

10. Quoted in John D. Hicks, *The Constitutions of the Northwest States* (Lincoln: University of Nebraska University Studies, 1923), 52.

11. Quoted in Morton Keller, *Affairs of State: Public Life in Nineteenth Century America* (Cambridge, Mass.: Belknap Press, 1977), 114.

12. Quoted in Daniel T. Rodgers, *Contested Truths: Keywords in American Politics Since Independence* (New York: Basic Books, 1987), 98.

13. These data are drawn from Albert L. Sturm, *Thirty Years of State Constitution-Making, 1938–1968* (New York: National Municipal League, 1970), 54, table 10.

14. See, for example, David Alan Johnson, *Founding the Far West: California, Oregon, and Nevada, 1840–1890* (Berkeley: University of California Press, 1992), and Gordon Bakken, *Rocky Mountain Constitution Making, 1850–1912* (Westport, Conn.: Greenwood Press, 1987).

15. 48 U.S. 1 (1849).

16. James Bryce, *The American Commonwealth* (Chicago: Charles H. Seagal, 1891), 1:394.

17. Quoted in Hicks, *Constitutions of the Northwest States*, 54 (italics added).

Index of Names